The Buy to Let Handbook

'An excellent first purchase for anyone contemplating investing in the buy to let market
whether they are proposing to manage the
property themselves or use an agent to do it
for them. First class and good value for
money.'
The Letting Centre (*Letting Update Journal*)

If you want to know how...

Making Money from Letting
How to buy and let residential property for profit

Save Thousands Buying Your Home
*A step-by-step guide to reducing the price of a house
and the cost of your mortgage*

Making Money from Holiday Lets
A start-up handbook for buying and letting holiday homes

Save Thousands Selling Your Home Yourself
*Use an estate agent's insider knowledge to sell your house
and save time and money*

Buy to Let Property Hotspots
Where to buy property and how to let it for profit

Property Hotspots in London
Where in our capital city to buy and let property for profit

howtobooks

Please send for a free copy of the latest catalogue to:

How To Books
3 Newtec Place, Magdalen Road
Oxford OX4 1RE, United Kingdom
email: info@howtobooks.co.uk
http://www.howtobooks.co.uk

The Buy to Let Handbook

How to invest for profit in residential

property and manage the letting yourself

TONY BOOTH

howtobooks

First published in 2003 by
How To Books Ltd, 3 Newtec Place
Magdalen Road, Oxford OX4 1RE. United Kingdom.
Tel: (01865) 793806. Fax: (01865) 248780.
email: info@howtobooks.co.uk
http://www.howtobooks.co.uk

First published 2003
Reprinted 2003
Reprinted 2004

British Library Cataloguing in Publication Data
A catalogue record for this book is available from the British
Library

Cover design by Baseline Arts Ltd, Oxford
Produced for How To Books by Deer Park Productions
Edited by Diana Brueton
Typeset by PDQ Typesetting, Newcastle-under-Lyme, Staffs.
Printed and bound by Cromwell Press Ltd, Trowbridge,
Wiltshire.

NOTE: The material contained in this book is set out in good
faith for general guidance and no liability can be accepted
for loss or expense incurred as a result of relying in particular
circumstances on statements made in the book. The laws and
regulations are complex and liable to change, and readers should
check the current position with the relevant authorities before
making personal arrangements.

Contents

List of Illustrations

Thank you for buying one of our books. We hope you'll enjoy the book, and that it will help you to invest in residential property – and make a profit.

We always try to ensure our books are up to date, but contact details seem to change so quickly that it can be very hard to keep up with them. If you do have any problems contacting any of the organisations listed at the back of the book please get in touch, and either we or the author will do what we can to help. And if you do find correct contact details that differ from those in the book, please let us know so that we can put it right when we reprint.

Please do also give us your feedback so we can go on making books that you want to read. If there's anything you particularly liked about this book – or you have suggestions about how it could be improved in the future – email us on info@howtobooks.co.uk

For further information on the property market you can subscribe to www.propertyhotspots.net for up to the minute information on property prices, property search, estate agents, letting agents, property auctions, 100% mortgage providers, buy to let mortgage providers and much more.

The Publishers
www.howtobooks.co.uk

Preface

Being a landlord has gained greater public acceptance today than at any other time in history. More people have achieved financial security in recent years and many have chosen to invest in or have inherited a second property. Letting is recognised as a reliable way of profiting from a second home and the practice has now become commonplace throughout all sections of society.

This recent and rapid escalation in the number of landlords has transformed the face of renting in England and Wales. The 1988 Housing Act was introduced by government to help fuel the rented sector by providing landlords and their tenants with a balanced degree of security. It created regulations to protect the landlord's income and guaranteed they would regain legal possession at the end of tenancy. It also provided tenants with good quality, safe housing and a defence against being evicted during the tenancy term.

With help from a stable and healthy economy and the resulting higher disposable income enjoyed by many, the residential letting market grew quickly. Although owner-occupiers are still in a majority, renting is seen as a viable and sometimes preferred alternative for many people. However, the modern landlord frequently lacks the experience, knowledge and time needed to deal efficiently with their property and tenants. Some jump in with both feet, blissfully ignorant of the laws affecting them, only to find themselves in deep and turbulent water within a very short period. It is perhaps not surprising that many resort to paying a letting agent to deal with the tenancy and, although some offer a very competent service, many fail to provide their clients with the personal care and attention ultimately desired.

This book intends to equip the reader with everything they need to know about buying and preparing a suitable investment property. It also explains how to find good tenants, where to obtain forms and how to complete tenancy agreements; it deals with deposits, rent arrears and the process of regaining possession. More importantly, it will help achieve compliance with the extensive volume of legislation affecting landlords in England and Wales. In short, it is a comprehensive but concise guide for the would-be, go-it-alone landlord wishing to evade agency fees by creating and managing their own tenancy.

After 20 years of being a landlord and operating as an estate agent and letting agent, I have concluded that knowledge provides much more than power... it allows the person possessing it to work efficiently, knowing they are armed against the pitfalls of ignorance. Minor hiccups will inevitably occur but, having a sound foundation in the standard of property being let, finding good tenants and having a comprehensive tenancy agreement all help reduce the risk.

By empowering yourself with the information in this book, you will enjoy the financial and personal rewards that becoming a landlord can provide. You will also have the satisfaction of knowing that you are in full control of who will occupy your most valued asset and for how long, the rent they will have to pay and the conditions they will need to observe. The private rented sector is an exciting, stimulating and challenging arena for novice and professional alike; this book will guide you through its many facets and show you how to generate a considerable income, even if you are currently employed in another occupation.

Throughout this book please note that for ease of reading the term *'landlord'* refers to either gender and to one or more people or to a company.

Tony Booth
e-mail: tony_booth@btopenworld.com

Acknowledgements

As always, thank you to my trusty band of proofreaders who have advised, suggested, criticised and edited much of the content of this book. I am particularly indebted to Chris Park and Alan Lancaster for giving freely of their time and expertise. Special thanks to Professor Peter Robson of the Law School at Strathclyde University, whose assistance in validating the chapter on Scottish law is much appreciated, and to the Scottish Executive for their help and advice.

1

Identifying a Suitable Property

In this chapter:

- ◆ recognising properties that are in demand
- ◆ researching local trends and facilities
- ◆ the potential of an investment property
- ◆ assessing leasehold restrictions
- ◆ avoiding a HiMO property
- ◆ essential elements to increase letting potential.

If you have yet to buy a property then you are in a very advantageous position as you can locate and purchase a unit that you know will be in demand. The only restrictions are likely to be the availability of such units and having enough funds to buy one. Failing to make a profit from letting is usually the result of poor planning and inadequate preparation. Many landlords make the mistake of trying to provide accommodation that is unsuitable for the area and only later discover there are not enough tenants available to maintain a high occupancy rate. The secret is to identify what is in demand and then endeavour to supply it.

RECOGNISING PROPERTIES THAT ARE IN DEMAND

Identifying your client group
There are two ways to do this depending on your personal circumstances and the preferred type of property and tenant.

◆ If you already have a preferred location, research the area thoroughly to assess the most likely type of tenant; this will help identify the most suitable type of property.

◆ If you have already decided on a particular type of tenant, examine where those tenants are most prevalent and buy appropriate property in that specific area.

In both situations, it is best to consult local estate agents who also operate as letting agents. They will advise on the best area to consider and the type of tenants seeking accommodation within it. This advice is usually free as they will see you as a potential future customer. Use their expertise as it could considerably increase your future profit margin. The following information may be helpful if you remain uncertain about your target client group.

Students

Students often seek low-cost accommodation close to their college or university and cohabit to reduce the burden of rent. This can be problematic if one of the group later decides to leave during the tenancy. It may be the student's first experience outside the parental home and the taste of freedom may result in excessive noise, untidiness and damage to property and décor. Landlords should consider supplying robust furnishings and ensure a parent acts as guarantor. Properties are likely to be in high demand during term-times only and may remain empty for periods in between. Before supplying student lets, confirm with the educational institution that a need exists for private sector dwellings as many provide their own subsidised accommodation on campus or nearby.

Tenants with young children

Terraced and semi-detached houses will be in high demand amongst this group providing they have adequate space and a safe enclosed garden area. Properties meeting the needs of a growing family are ideal, particularly those located near a school, recreation space, health centre and neighbourhood shops. Good public transport routes are also often desired.

The unemployed and/or those in receipt of housing benefit

Bear in mind that *anyone* can become suddenly unemployed and may therefore need to apply for housing benefit. That said, supplying specifically to those in receipt of benefit is *not* a course advised for the novice landlord. The benefit system is very complex and fraught with problems. Even experienced landlords are often frustrated by delayed benefit payments, unhelpful local authority staff, red tape and bureaucracy. Landlords are advised to obtain information from the local authority about housing benefit and to consult experienced landlords through local forums or associations.

Employed young couples

By far the greatest number and diversity of tenants seeking rented property of all types are young single people or couples in full-time employment. This is the ideal group to target as there will be fewer problems encountered before, during and at the end of a tenancy. The type of property best to supply will vary according to:

◆ employment opportunities in the area
◆ the income and aspirations of tenants
◆ and the facilities afforded by the neighbourhood.

Elderly tenants

In general, elderly tenants focus on different elements from younger people when looking for rented accommodation. Matters important to them will include:

* ease of access
* good and courteous neighbours
* security and safety
* good public transport
* and plenty of local facilities all within easy reach.

In contrast, properties:

* above the first floor with no elevator
* located in an area with a high crime rate
* with a younger age population
* or lacking security measures

are likely to discourage the elderly. This is a good group to target if a suitable property can be found, as most elderly tenants:

* care for their accommodation
* pay their rent in full and on time and
* tend to repeatedly renew contracts over a long period.

The disabled

The term 'disabled' encompasses a wide group of people, many of whom are poorly catered for in the private sector. This gap in provision can be filled successfully and profitably by landlords prepared to meet the needs of this group. Approach the local authority, social services, nearby hospitals, and also any appropriate charity or agency, to assess the level of demand and appropriate requirements.

Remember that, in providing a property to this group, you will have to ensure it is adapted to meet the needs of the individual and that it conforms to both local and national guidelines for health and safety (you or the tenant may be entitled to grant-aid for any necessary adaptations).

Young professional high-earners

This is a good group to target if you can acquire the right property in a sophisticated and fashionable area or a luxury residence close to a city centre. Young professional high-earners (YPHEs) rarely rent for more than two or three years in any location because they have a career strategy and frequently pursue improved positions elsewhere in the country. However, whilst occupying your property they are prepared to pay a high rent and will care appropriately for the accommodation. The only problems to consider are that YPHEs:

◆ have high expectations about the quality and location of the property

◆ are concerned about the calibre of furnishings and standard of decoration

◆ will demand a superior level of service from you as their landlord.

Any faults reported must be dealt with fast and efficiently. The initial capital outlay for a suitable property will be considerable but, given its location in a good area, it should achieve above-average capital growth by the time you sell it. Meanwhile, you can anticipate a reasonable return through letting.

Company lettings

Consider targeting major employers in the region with details of your property. With a company let it is the business that is named on the tenancy agreement instead of an individual person. This type of tenancy has several advantages for the landlord:

- rent payments are usually made promptly by bank standing order

- tenancies are often renewed over several years

- any damage is usually dealt with quickly and professionally.

Companies invariably look for well maintained units at competitive rents and with a superior management service. A company letting can pay dividends if you and your chosen property can fulfil these requirements.

RESEARCHING LOCAL TRENDS AND FACILITIES

Buying close to home

If possible, choose a property near to or within easy reach of where you live. Apart from giving you some peace of mind it also means you will:

- have good local knowledge to answer tenant enquiries

- be within easy reach for viewing appointments, emergency

repairs and to undertake regular inspections of the property

◆ recognise when the area is deteriorating to assess the best time to sell.

Local information

Find out all you can about the neighbourhood where you are considering buying property and try to match the facilities available with your chosen client group. It is rare to find an ideal *property* in a perfect *location* at an acceptable *price*, but confirming the greatest number of positive elements under each heading will produce mutually satisfying results for you and your future tenants.

Supply and demand are the greatest influences involved in letting. They affect the length of time a property will be let (without void periods) and the rent achievable. Assess demand by talking to letting agents who will have a unique insight into their area. Assess supply (and any potential over-supply) by looking at 'to let' boards in the neighbourhood and advertisements in local newspapers. Check the same boards and adverts weekly to see how quickly properties are being let.

Ask the local authority planning department about new developments under construction or any that are being proposed. What changes are likely to take place in the locality? Will they adversely affect your ability to let a property nearby?

Examine the number of major employers in the area and identify any proposals for land redevelopment. A new hospital being built will attract a growing local population. Staff will need somewhere to live and this increase in demand could sustain your property for several years. Conversely, a factory announcing closure might be symptomatic of a local recession. Property may be devalued as a result and there could be an over-supply of rented accommodation in the long term.

THE POTENTIAL OF AN INVESTMENT PROPERTY

Apartments -v- houses

If the demand exists and you are able to quantify it, invest in an apartment rather than a house. The main reasons for this are:

- apartments attract a mobile population and are always in high demand, particularly in city-centre areas;

- apartments require less maintenance, reducing annual expenditure;

- apartments are usually less expensive to buy and easier to sell;

- upper floor apartments are more secure during void periods;

- apartments generally occupy less space and therefore require less furniture, carpets and equipment;

- a garden will require attention during void periods; an apartment balcony will not.

However, bear in mind:

- in rural areas, small family houses with a garden may be in higher demand than apartments;

- apartment blocks may have a service charge for maintenance and common area upkeep which will have to be paid whether the property is occupied or not;

- the enjoyment of an apartment is dependent on there being thoughtful neighbours above, below and to each side;

- the cleanliness, decoration and general condition of the external aspects and communal entrance hallways will be controlled by the management company, whereas with a house the owner is usually directly in control;

- apartment owners are often prohibited from letting their property by the lease (but see below).

Investment property

'Investment property' is a title often given to dwellings that need considerable repair. They may appear attractive to the novice landlord simply because of their low price but buyers of this type of property need to be aware that:

- A comprehensive survey is essential before submitting an offer, so that all defects are identified and realistic costs of repair can be obtained from contractors.

- There will be a void period from the day of purchase to repairs being completed when no income will be earned. Despite this, there may be charges to you as the owner for council tax, electricity, gas, service charge and/or management-fees, which will have to be paid from personal funds.

- The property may be in a run-down area with neighbouring properties in a comparable poor condition and this will reduce the long-term letting potential.

◆ It may be difficult to obtain a mortgage, as most lenders will not want to accept the risk of repairs being completed. Any loan granted is therefore likely to be low and the lender may also require additional security.

◆ The investment property may be classed as a HiMO (see below) and lack the minimum fire-safety and other standards required for such dwellings. Some landlords are now disposing of these properties, with vacant possession and at a low market value, to evade the long-term improvement costs.

ASSESSING LEASEHOLD RESTRICTIONS

Leasehold properties

Where a property is leasehold, the owner ('lessee') must abide by the conditions of the lease. Leases are usually for a term of 999 years (or the remainder of) for older properties, but can be for the remainder of 99 or even 50 years for many newly built inner city dwellings. Once the lease expires, the property ownership usually reverts to the headlessor. Mortgage lenders are often reluctant to advance a loan for any purchase where the lease is 50 years or less because the property value reduces according to the shortened lease-term remaining.

The lease should always be thoroughly inspected *before* purchase as many prohibit letting. If such a clause exists, write to the headlessor and enquire whether owners are allowed to conditionally let (or more accurately sub-let). When an arrangement of this type is made, there is sometimes an additional charge to the owner which may be a single or an annual payment or a charge per tenancy. Bear in mind that these additional expenses reduce annual letting profit.

The lease may also prohibit your tenant from keeping pets, disturbing neighbours with noise after a certain time, erecting a satellite dish or TV aerial, and many other restrictions. As the owner, you will be responsible for *ensuring* your tenants keep to these conditions.

AVOIDING A HiMO PROPERTY

Houses in multiple occupation (HiMOs)

The novice landlord should be extremely cautious before contemplating the purchase of a 'House in Multiple Occupation (HiMO)' – or of letting an ordinary house and, by virtue of the manner in which it is let, allowing it to become a HiMO. The problem is that this type of property must conform to a vast array of rules and regulations, some of which are nationally enforced, others are specified by particular local authorities.

Some local authorities are extremely stringent and, if they believe a HiMO fails to meet the minimum standards of safety and management, they can force compliance through registration and statutory notice and even close a property down, if the landlord fails to make the necessary changes within a given time.

A 'HiMO' is a dwelling *'occupied by persons who do not form a single household'*. Ordinarily, this is likely to be a property converted into bedsits, small flats or rooms, with shared facilities such as a kitchen, bathroom, entrance, etc. But some local authorities include any dwelling where three or more unrelated people are sharing. For more information, consult the Local Authority Environmental Health Officer for the area where you are considering a purchase. Also, obtain a copy of the *Housing (Management of Houses in Multiple Occupation) Regulations 1990* from a local HMSO (telephone 020 7873 9090 for details). There is an excellent Internet site at **www.landlordzone.co.uk** for additional reading on this and other relevant subjects and for an overview of the regulations.

The definition of, and approach to, HiMOs by different local authorities has been the subject of debate and contention amongst landlords, tenants, solicitors and other agencies for over a decade. The government is currently reviewing the regulations affecting HiMOs in England and Wales to clarify the situation, though some commentators anticipate tighter controls and a compulsory national registration scheme for HiMO landlords.

ESSENTIAL ELEMENTS TO INCREASE LETTING POTENTIAL

There are specific elements of a property that increase its letting potential. Although these will vary according to the individual location and certain tenant groups, many are universally desired by those seeking new accommodation. Examine the following and attempt to acquire a property combining most of the components listed (not in any preferred order):

Houses	Apartments
attractive location	attractive and fashionable location
private and safe garden	well-maintained communal grounds
secure garage	secure garage or designated bay

double-glazed windows	double-glazed windows
modern kitchen and bathroom	modern kitchen and bathroom
gas central heating	gas central heating
separate shower cubicle	quality soundproof timber flooring
quality alarm system	quality alarm system
spacious living room	above ground floor
log or coal-burning fire	some storage space
south-facing garden	south-facing balcony
conservatory	lift access to upper floors
original quality features	modern hi-tech features
neutral décor	neutral décor
fitted bedrooms	fitted bedrooms
guest WC	en-suite shower
good commuting position	good public transport route
quiet roads (safe for children)	close to or in a city centre location

Who is selling and why?

Find out as much as you can about the seller and do not be afraid to ask why they are selling. The owner will be aware of any adverse conditions affecting the neighbourhood (and the property) and, although they are unlikely to freely divulge this information to a potential buyer, the way they respond may suggest you should be more cautious about proceeding.

An effective method is to knock on a few doors of neighbouring properties and politely explain that you are considering a purchase. Ask if they would be prepared to advise you about any known problems with the area and properties in it. The information given by this method has proved invaluable in my own property investments; in my experience, first-hand local knowledge should always be considered paramount when planning a purchase.

SUMMARY

♦ Choose a location that is popular for letting and with an abundance of eager tenants.

♦ Identify your target client group, learn their housing needs and supply them.

♦ Apartments are more popular than houses, particularly in cities, but find out what type of property people are looking for in your own area.

♦ Read any lease governing the property thoroughly before purchase to find out whether letting is prohibited.

♦ Take into account the full and real cost in time and money to undertake repairs and improvements to an investment property.

♦ Be cautious of buying a HiMO.

♦ When choosing a property to buy, assess whether it has enough good qualities to optimise its future letting potential.

(2)

Buying the Property

In this chapter:

- estimating running costs
- assessing and forecasting the yield
- taxation
- buying with tenants in occupation
- surveying the property
- finding a competitive mortgage
- investing with substantial existing capital
- timing is everything!

Having found a property, you need to examine its income potential more carefully and consider the options for buying it. Rushing in will simply invite disaster. Bear in mind that, once you have bought the property, it must work *for* you, not *against* you! Take your time and research thoroughly. Make a plan of how you intend to proceed. Consider matters such as:

- funding
- instructing a solicitor experienced in let property
- obtaining a survey
- making essential repairs
- assessing rental income after expenses
- undertaking legally required inspections
- buying furniture and equipment
- acquiring tenants and obtaining references for them.

You should only consider submitting an offer to purchase if you feel confident about the above elements.

ESTIMATING RUNNING COSTS

It may be difficult to identify all the costs associated with letting a property *before* purchase, particularly if it has not been let before. Some expenses may have to be estimated and a rent level calculated from limited information.

The exercise is nonetheless essential if you are to quantify the income-generating potential of your proposed investment. Remember that it must make a reasonable profit after all deductions to produce a favourable income. Failing to do this could mean squandering time and effort on an unproductive venture.

Occupied running costs

'Occupied' running costs are items you will have to pay with tenants living in the dwelling. These include:

- Mortgage payments.

- Lender's authorisation fee (letting is usually prohibited by mortgage lenders but permission may be given subject to a charge per tenancy term).

- Accountant's fees.

- Bank charges.

- Legal charges if a solicitor deals with the tenancy agreement, otherwise the cost of purchased forms (allow £50 a year).

- Tenant referencing.

- Stamp duty payments (allow £10 per year for two six-month tenancies if rent is likely to be in excess of £5,000 per term).

- Minor repairs (allow 10% of rent over 12 months as a mean average).

- Council tax if the property is a HiMO.

- Water charges (normally paid by the tenant but some water companies impose the charge on the landlord; check with the water company for your area).

- Replacements and renewals for carpets, furnishings, fittings and equipment (allow 10% of rent over 12 months).

- Building insurance (some policies do not offer cover to let property and block policies offered through service-charge payments rarely provide adequate protection to landlords).

- Landlord's contents insurance (some policies do not offer cover to let properties or between tenancies or for those considered to be a high-risk, for example HiMOs and student lets).

- Any management or service charge payable (the owner/long-lessee is always liable, it is rare for management companies to provide for the sub-tenant to meet such charges).

- Gas-safety inspections which are legally required and must be conducted by a CORGI (Council of Registered Gas Installers) engineer.

- Electrical safety inspections (ideally conducted prior to each tenancy term or otherwise annually). A five-year check of wiring and system installations is considered good practice.

◆ Other expenses, such as the use of a car to get to and from the property, telephone, postage, stationery, photographs for inventories, copying keys and photocopying manuals and documents.

Unoccupied running costs

'Unoccupied' running costs are items you will need to pay when the dwelling is empty. These are likely to include:

◆ Gas and electricity charges for heating and lighting (heating will be needed in cold weather and lighting will be required for viewings and/or whilst undertaking maintenance). Allow two monthly payments per year.

◆ Council tax (at a reduced rate for empty properties). Allow two monthly payments per year.

◆ Interior decorating and exterior painting (a considerable expense if a contractor is hired).

◆ Cleaning (labour and materials); allow for pre-tenancy and post-tenancy cleaning. Allow for professional carpet cleaning every two years.

◆ Gardening (when the property is empty). Add an element for the upkeep of any garage, outbuilding, fencing or walls.

◆ Tenant advertising (or tenant-find agency charges).

◆ TV licence (if a television set is provided).

Estimating the rent level

Complete the following three exercises:

1. Invite local letting agents to view your property and assess an appropriate monthly rent. This service is usually free of charge as they will hope you will employ them.

2. Examine local newspapers to see what rents are being advertised for similar properties in the area.

3. Walk around the neighbourhood and identify any 'to let' boards. Obtain the full details of each property and note the rent of any dwellings comparable to the one you are proposing to purchase.

From this you should be able to make a realistic estimate of the appropriate rent for your property.

ASSESSING AND FORECASTING THE YIELD

'Yield' is a term used by property investors to calculate the profitability of different dwellings in the letting market. Most landlords recognise two distinct types of profit involved with property: short-term **'income from letting'** and long-term **'capital growth'**. The yield, expressed as a percentage, takes both into consideration to provide a comprehensive assessment and 6% to 9% is acceptable to most landlords.

With the information obtained so far, you can calculate the yield with the formula in Figure 1.

$$\frac{\text{(a) Net Letting Profit (after tax)}}{\substack{\text{(b) Current Property Value} \\ \text{(less selling costs)}}} \times 100 = \text{(c) Yield (\%)}$$

Fig. 1. Yield calculation.

Enter the data you have obtained into the document below. Repeat this for each property.

INCOME	Year 1	Year 2	Year 3
(a) Rent anticipated per month			
(b) Number of months per year the property is likely to be let			
(c) Rental INCOME per year ('a' multiplied by 'b')			
EXPENSES			
Mortgage (interest element only can be offset against tax)			
Lender's administration fees			
Accountancy fees			
Bank charges			
Legal fees including tenancy forms			
Tenant referencing			
Stamp duty			
Minor repairs and maintenance			
Council tax (if a HiMO)			
Water charges			
Replacements and renewals			
Insurance			
Management/service charge			
Gas and electrical safety inspections			
Void period gas, electricity, council tax, water, TV licence			
Painting and decorating			
Cleaning			
Advertising			
Gardening			
Other: travel, postage, stationery, keys, photocopying			
(d) Total EXPENSES			
(e) Taxable profit ('c' less 'd')			
(f) Tax at __% =			
(g) PROFIT AFTER TAX ('e' less 'f')			
YIELD (divide 'g' by the current saleable value after deducting all estimated selling costs, then multiply by 100)			

Fig. 2. Record of forecasted profit.

Yield can change from year to year according to the value of the property, the rent obtained and the level of expenses incurred through letting. By applying this approach to several properties you can identify which is the better-buy at any particular point in time.

Professional investors forecast the anticipated yield over several years and you can also attempt this by taking advice and making considered·judgements about expenses, tax liability, rental income and property value. The ambition of all speculators is to see the yield rise above the best interest-rate return from a bank or building society or other forms of investment. Buying a low-maintenance property in a good area, at a competitive price and with the qualities required to produce a good letting income, will help to achieve a yield of between 7% and 10%.

The calculation models described in this section are examples only, given for guidance. Other models with variable formulae may produce different results. It is not possible here to take into account the various elements which may be pertinent to your personal circumstances.

TAXATION

Income tax

You will be liable to pay income tax on the profit made from letting, after deducting any allowable expenses. The way tax is calculated will vary according to personal circumstances, any additional sources of income and other elements influencing your financial situation. You should:

◆ Make contact with your local tax office at the earliest opportunity, explain your plans and seek advice. The tax office will help you estimate the tax you are likely to pay from letting.

◆ Keep all receipts, paid invoices and any relevant documents relating to the property, as these will be required when completing your accounts for the Inland Revenue. Keep a record of the date paid, how it was paid and brief details of the service or materials bought.

◆ Consider employing an accountant *before* you buy the property. An experienced and qualified accountant will be able to offer you good advice and save you money in the long term.

◆ Take a course on book-keeping. You need to know how to keep adequate records for both the Inland Revenue and for your accountant. Presenting your records properly will also help to reduce accountancy costs.

◆ On the Internet, the Revenue's own Website at **www.inlandrevenue.gov.uk** offers lots of useful advice and a list of local offices. **www.digita.com** includes a tax calculator, up-to-date news, information relating to taxation, and a question and answer forum.

Capital gains tax

Capital gains tax (CGT) is not usually payable on an individual's own home. It is, however, payable on most let property. You are liable to CGT on the profit made from selling it, that is, the capital remaining after deducting the original purchase price and accounting for personal allowances and permitted expenses whilst owned. CGT rules change occasionally. Your accountant will advise you about the current situation and suggest the best arrangements for buying the property to reduce your eventual liability to CGT.

BUYING WITH TENANTS IN OCCUPATION

Proceed with extreme caution if considering the purchase of a dwelling with existing tenants. Give regard to the following:

◆ Obtain copies of the tenancy agreements and any notices issued. Consult a solicitor experienced in the legal aspects of letting to confirm that agreements have been properly completed and conform to current Housing Act legislation.

◆ Obtain copies of the inventories, gas safety certificates, any record of electrical safety inspections, and any other appropriate documentation relating to the property and occupiers.

◆ Obtain the original referencing results and ask for details of any rent arrear history.

◆ Confirm that the current occupiers of the property are those named on the tenancy agreements (for example, has a vacated sharer been replaced or has a tenant now got an unidentified partner living with them).

◆ Identify the term for each tenancy (it may affect your ability to gain vacant possession if no term exists or one has expired).

◆ Read the tenancy agreements, giving particular attention to landlord obligations and facilities to increase rents.

◆ Meet the occupiers and satisfy yourself that these are the type of people you would have chosen as tenants.

- If in doubt, ask the seller whether he would be willing to offer the property with vacant possession (that is, buy only after all tenants have vacated).

Buying with existing furnishings

It may appear advantageous to buy a property already furnished and equipped. However, it will be uneconomic if furnishings and equipment are of a poor quality and/or do not comply with current legislation. Read Chapter 3 before proceeding, otherwise you may find yourself paying additionally for disposal costs.

SURVEYING THE PROPERTY

Inspecting the fabric of the building

As an estate agent, it often surprises me that so few people inspect properties thoroughly before buying them. Don't allow the seller to intimidate you. Remember, they are asking you to hand over a considerable sum for their property. Take your time and scrutinise the building thoroughly. When inspecting:

- Take notes about any adverse observations.

- Be prepared for every eventuality: take a small pair of step-ladders for access to the roof space, binoculars to view the exterior and socket-testers to check for faulty wiring (available at most good DIY stores).

- Check all window frames internally and externally for rot and confirm that they all open properly.

- Look for condensation between the two panes of glass with any double-glazing. This is evidence of a broken seal.

- Check all accessible water-pipes for leaks and confirm that pipes and tanks in the loft or in a cellar are lagged.

- Inspect baths, basins, showers, toilets and cisterns for cracks, dripping taps, leaks, poor seals, mould-growth and other damage. Turn taps and extractors on to ensure proper operation. Give particular attention to the area beneath hot and cold water tanks where staining may indicate an ongoing or old leak.

- Gently tap ceramic tiled walls to identify any that are loose.

- Pull back carpets where possible to assess the condition of the flooring.

- As you go through a doorway, close the door to ensure it fits correctly in the frame.

- Inspect ceilings for bowing as this is a sign of loose plaster. Look also for leakage stains.

- Examine the exterior for blocked, damaged or missing sections of guttering; broken slabs or paving that rises above the damp-proof course; missing or damaged roof slates; crumbling brickwork and receding mortar joints; damage to boundary walls or rickety fencing; and look inside any garage, shed or outbuilding.

Arranging for a survey to be undertaken

Once you have conducted your own in-depth inspection of the building and are reasonably content with its condition, invest in a more professional and comprehensive surveyor's report. Before proceeding check with your mortgage company, as many require you use an approved or in-house surveyor.

If you are happy with the results, consider employing an electrician to check the property's electrical system (see also Chapter 3). It is also prudent to employ a plumber to inspect water-pipes, taps, stop-cocks, radiators, tanks, pumps and boilers.

FINDING A COMPETITIVE MORTGAGE

There is a vast array of mortgages available and the variation can be very confusing. The Financial Services Authority (FSA) is the independent watchdog set up by government to regulate financial services and protect the rights of the public. It provides a free, plain English *Guide to Mortgages* which can be obtained by writing to them at 25 The North Colonnade, Canary Wharf, London E14 5HS (telephone 0845 606 1234 or visit **www.fsa.gov.uk/consumer**).

Once you have decided the best type of mortgage, you can start searching for one that provides the best value. The internet is an easy way of obtaining up-to-date information and you can access thousands of loans offered by lenders throughout the country. If you are able to let your computer do the walking, try these sites:

www.moneysupermarket.com for advice on the best-buy mortgage in various categories. Their *Rate Alert* system updates you by e-mail when a better interest-rated mortgage enters the market.

www.moneyextra.com/compare/mortgages to search through over 4,000 different mortgages.

www.yourmortgage.co.uk supplies mortgage information and current 'best buy' details with advice for the self-employed.

www.mortgagesexposed.com is a quite extraordinary website offering a free on-line or downloadable book covering every aspect of the subject.

One alternative to using the internet is to consult a mortgage broker. There are mortgages not generally advertised and better deals that a broker has access to. They will identify a selection that best meets your circumstances. Brokers charge for their services so find out what fees are involved before employing one. A list of mortgage brokers can be found in *Yellow Pages* or consult your accountant who may be able to recommend a local one to you.

How To Books have published *Save Thousands Buying Your Home* by Maxwell Hodson. This is an excellent reference and guide for anyone considering a property purchase. Alongside useful money-saving information, it offers the reader realistic, sound advice on how to obtain the lowest mortgage and arrange finances so you get the best deal.

Before accepting a mortgage, obtain written confirmation from the lender that letting is permitted. Some completely prohibit renting. Others may have strict rules about the category of tenant, the type of tenancy agreement and the method of management. There are also often mandatory fees payable to mortgage companies for granting a tenancy and these are best identified in advance so you can include them in any profit forecast.

Buy-to-let mortgages

In recent years, lenders have recognised that many people wish to invest in property intended for the letting market. Some have devised products specifically tailored to would-be landlords (called 'buy-to-let' schemes). The concept was originally promoted by ARLA (the Association of Residential Letting Agents) whose members reported a gap in the availability of mortgages for their client landlords. Buy to let packages, varying in nature, can now be obtained from many high-street lenders, including most banks and building societies.

The advantages include:

- The letting income generated by the property forms part of the decision-making calculation by the lender for granting an advance.

- Lenders are usually prepared to consider granting a mortgage, even though the applicant may already have one running on their own home.

- Those who are self-employed (or intending to be full-time landlords) and those otherwise unemployed are not usually obstructed from making an application.

The disadvantages include:

- Lenders usually require a significant amount of information about the property and forecasted data on the anticipated rental income.

- It may be compulsory to accept various insurance policies from the lender.

- The tenancy agreement must be drawn up by a solicitor or through a recognised agency.

- It is often mandatory to employ a letting agent approved by the lender to oversee the creation and management of the tenancy.

For more details about buy to let, visit ARLA's website on the subject: **www.buytolet.co.uk**. Alternatively, consult any high-street bank for details of their package and shop around because schemes vary from one lender to another.

INVESTING WITH SUBSTANTIAL EXISTING CAPITAL
If you have substantial capital, you may be tempted to buy a property outright without considering the advantages of a loan. You may believe that full ownership is safer, easier and more rewarding, as it will negate third-party involvement and minimise complications. Whilst all of that is true. . .you could also be reducing the potential return from your investment! With capital of between £100,000 and £200,000 or more, you are able to enter the realm of the serious let-property investor and achieve potential high returns from a process known as **gearing**.

As the term implies, gearing is a means of *getting out* more than you *put in*. It allows you to acquire more properties through planned and careful investment, using the capital to obtain additional funds. The more properties in your port-folio, the more income can be generated through letting *and*, by buying the right properties and selling them at the right time, the more capital growth you can make. The more capital you have the more you can invest. . .and so on. Some of the most successful millionaires have made their fortune this way.

There is a higher degree of risk involved, but then the potential returns are higher too. Success lies in the breadth of knowledge and experience that the investor has about property in general. They must have an eye for dwellings with potential for capital growth and understand when it is right to buy and wise to sell. They need a sound business plan and access to skilled financial advisors. They must also be capable of accepting risks in their investment strategy.

When gearing is used to good effect, a yield of up to 20% or more can be achieved, given an element of luck in finding the right properties in the right location, purchased at good prices and sold when local values are at their highest. Add to this low void periods, good tenants, high rents and prolonged low interest rates, and the return on capital can be multiplied several times over. Always bear in mind that gearing brings a better return when the total yield plus capital growth exceeds the borrowing rate, that is, the cost of acquiring funds.

www.mortgagesexposed.com/Book_Contents/buytolet.htm on the internet has one of the best plain English explanations of the subject I have found in recent years. For more in-depth reading, you may wish to obtain *Buy to Let Secrets* by Richard Davies and Neil Lewis, which offers comprehensive and stimulating information on the topic (JoJaffa Ltd. Tel: 020 8715 3525).

An inherited property

Acquiring an inheritance in the form of property can be advantageous, but only if it conforms to all the criteria for letting so far outlined. There is little point in having a golden chalice, if there is no fitting use for it. The property may be in the wrong location or lack appropriate qualities for letting. Consider the merits of selling it to finance a more suitable acquisition elsewhere. Bear in mind that selling will involve additional costs and potential liability for capital gains tax. Consult your accountant before taking action as the timing of a sale and subsequent purchase can influence the degree of liability.

TIMING IS EVERYTHING!

Time really *does* cost money, and this is no more certain than in the period from receiving the keys for your property to having tenants occupying it. Make every attempt to reduce lost income by manipulating the completion date to fall in line with your plans. If repairs are needed make certain that your contractors are *ready to go*; have decorators on stand-by; have furnishings and appliances identified and have adequate funds available to purchase them.

If possible, arrange for completion to occur during good letting months and **not** just before Christmas or during very cold and wet periods. Undertake as much as possible in advance so that once you have the keys you can get the property earning money for you.

SUMMARY

- ◆ Assess each property carefully before you purchase. Calculate and compare running costs and the forecasted yield to identify the best buy.

- ◆ Be aware of how your tax liability will influence profit.

- Inspect the building's fabric and arrange a survey so that defects and repair costs can be properly evaluated.

- Research the best method of funding your investment. Use the internet and/or a mortgage broker to find the best deal available. Before accepting a mortgage, check that letting is permitted and identify any associated charges or mandatory procedures.

- Organise as much as possible ahead of purchase to prevent losing income through having an empty dwelling.

Legally Required
Pre-Letting Inspections

In this chapter:

- how the law will affect you
- electrical safety legislation
- gas safety legislation
- furnishings legislation
- fire safety legislation
- health and safety issues.

HOW THE LAW WILL AFFECT YOU

Landlords in England and Wales must comply with a large volume of legislation. Failure to do so can lead to severe fines and even imprisonment. Some landlords flout the law foolishly believing they will not get caught; others do so out of ignorance. Either way, they run the risk of losing their entire business and, where culpable injury has occurred, their freedom too.

To comply with current Regulations, the following inspections *must* be conducted *before* a property is tenanted.

ELECTRICAL SAFETY LEGISLATION

Although there is no statutory requirement to have rented property formally inspected for electrical safety at set periods, landlords are legally required to provide a dwelling that is safe. The laws affecting them include:

♦ The Electrical Equipment (Safety) Regulations 1994
♦ The Plugs and Sockets (Safety) Regulations 1994
♦ The Consumer Protection Act 1987
♦ The Low Voltage Electrical Equipment Regulations 1989
♦ The General Product Safety Regulations 1994.

Some of these regulations only affect letting agents and those who rent property commercially or for business. There is debate about whether individual landlords letting a single dwelling without an agent must comply with all of them. However, as failing to comply can result in fines of up to £5,000 per offence, up to six months' imprisonment, being sued by the tenant for civil damages and, in the event of a death occurring, possible manslaughter charges, it is better to observe them and feel confident about your letting.

A wise landlord will employ a qualified electrician for an initial and further periodic inspections, producing a test report which can later be attached to the inventory. Ideally, the inspection should be carried out prior to each tenancy commencing, or at least annually. To become compliant, the following are recommended:

♦ Check that all appliance manuals, instructions, safety notices and labels are available so that copies can be issued to tenants.

♦ Have a qualified electrician check that all appliances are safely wired and operate properly.

- Do not buy second-hand electrical goods unless you can prove they are safe and have the appropriate instructions.

- Check that appliances have no damaged, worn or loose cables and that plugs are securely fitted and properly fused.

- Check that plugs and sockets conform to BS1363 or BS1363/A.

- Make certain that appropriate appliances are earthed.

- Have a qualified electrician inspect the property wiring (power and lighting), earthing, sockets, switches and fusing system, to ensure they meet current regulations and operate properly.

- Remember to inspect *all* areas of the property, including any attic or loft space, garage, outbuilding, shed and garden, and any appliances in them.

Copies of these and other Regulations can be obtained from a local HMSO or by writing to The Stationery Office, PO Box 29, St Crispins House, Duke Street, Norwich NR3 1PD. Tel: 0870 600 5522. Website: **www.hmso.gov.uk**

GAS SAFETY LEGISLATION
The law affecting individual landlords with regard to gas safety is more absolute than for electrical safety. It includes:

- The Gas Safety (Installation and Use) Regulations 1998
- The Gas Cooking Appliances (Safety) Regulations 1989.

Part of the landlord's statutory duty involves arranging for an annual gas safety inspection by a CORGI (Council for Registered Gas Installers) registered engineer. Failure to comply is a criminal offence and a fine of up to £5,000 and/or six months' imprisonment can be imposed. In serious cases civil proceedings can also be brought against the landlord. The Regulations include requirements that a landlord must:

- Ensure there is no open-flue gas appliance in any bedroom or any room where people may sleep, a bathroom or shower-room.

- Ensure that any work to or installation of gas appliances, fittings or equipment is conducted by a CORGI registered installer.

- Ensure that both fixed and mobile gas appliances and associated pipes and flues are safely maintained and that a formal safety inspection is conducted at least once a year by a CORGI registered installer.

- Ensure that, following any work to any gas appliance, a CORGI registered engineer conducts a defined series of tests to guarantee safety.

- Give tenants access to all appropriate manuals, safety notices and labels, and all instructions, for any gas appliance supplied.

- Keep adequate records of gas appliances including the dates of formal inspections and details of any defects identified and work required or conducted. A copy of the records must be made available to the tenant within 28 days of the inspection or prior to occupation if it is a new tenancy.

- Keep safety inspection reports and certificates issued by a CORGI installer for a minimum of two years.

- Prevent tenants from using any gas appliance where its safety or proper installation is suspect or a fault known.

In addition, landlords are advised to make tenants fully aware of *their* obligations under the Regulations which include:

- They must not interfere with, add to or otherwise conduct any work on any gas appliance, installation or associated pipes.

- They must inform the landlord immediately if they suspect a fault.

- They must take appropriate emergency action according to the situation. If they smell gas or suspect an appliance or installation to be dangerous, they should turn the gas supply off at the main cut-off valve and inform TRANSCO straight away. This authority does not sell gas but maintains a 24 hour emergency service for gas escape (Tel: 0800 111999).

- They should provide access to the property, given reasonable notice in writing, for the landlord's engineer to conduct the annual gas safety inspection.

- They should not introduce to the property any mobile or fixed gas appliance known or suspected to be faulty.

When arranging for a gas safety inspection, ask the engineer for a CORGI identification-card number and registration number. To verify the authenticity of their registration, call CORGI on 01256 372300 or visit the internet website at

www.corgi-gas.com Visitors to the site can also locate an engineer in their area. Copies of the Gas Safety Regulations can be obtained from a local HMSO or by writing to the Stationery Office or going on-line to **www.hmso.gov.uk**

Landlords should consider offering their tenants a defence against the potentially fatal consequences of carbon-mon-oxide (CO) poisoning. CO is produced through inadequate combustion of solid, gas or liquid fuels, usually due to faulty or badly installed appliances and blocked or damaged flues. Installing a carbon-monoxide alarm provides an effective early-warning system. Units can be bought for about £30 from good DIY stores.

FURNISHINGS LEGISLATION

Landlords must ensure that furnishings meet the standards enforced under current regulations. The effective legislation includes:

◆ The Furniture and Furnishings (Fire) (Safety) Regulations 1988 (amended in 1989 and 1993)
◆ The Consumer Protection Act 1987.

Some professionals question whether an individual land-lord letting a property on a one-off short-term basis, and not as part of a business, needs to comply with these Reg-ulations. Interpretation of the law is a matter for the courts; however, landlords must consider the repercussions of fail-ing to comply. The penalties include a fine of £5,000 per item not complying and/or six months' imprisonment. The consequences resulting from injury or death of a tenant are much more serious. Remember that, unless you receive professional legal advice before letting the property, your liability status may at best be precarious. Novice landlords should therefore err on the side of caution by verifying that furnishings comply. The Regulations were brought into force following numerous deaths caused by fire and smoke inhalation from foam-filled and other furnishings. Manufacturers are legally bound to produce safe products and all furnishings purchased new should comply with the minimum legal requirements. This fact does not, however, offer a landlord any degree of certainty in complying.

A landlord must supply only approved goods and have evidence that the appropriate labels are affixed to them. Examples of display labels and permanent labels are shown in Figures 3 and 4; the Regulations contain full-size colour illustrations. Landlords must examine the actual Regulations for reference purposes.

Items that must comply include:

- three-piece suites, armchairs and sofas
- futons, bed settees and other 'convertible' furnishings
- beds and bed bases as well as mattresses, headboards and pillows
- cushions and fitted or loose seating, pillows and pads
- stretch, loose and fitted covers for furniture
- dining and kitchen chairs with upholstered seats, backs or arms
- nursery furniture including baby chairs, cots and changing mats
- garden furniture containing upholstery that might be used indoors.

Filling material(s) and covering
fabric(s) meet the requirements
for resistance to cigarette and
match ignition in
the 1988 safety regulations

**CARELESSNESS
CAUSES FIRE**

RESISTANT

Fig. 3. Example of a furniture display label.

CARELESSNESS
CAUSES FIRE

A N Other Ltd. AB1 2XY

AB 1234

1 March 1990

**This article contains CM Foam
which passes the specified test.
All upholstery is cigarette resistant.**

All cover fabric is cotton and is match resistant.

This article does not include a
Schedule 3 interliner.

Fig. 4. Example of a permanent furniture label.

Specifically excluded are:

- carpets
- curtains
- loose mattress covers
- pillow cases
- sleeping bags
- antique furniture or furniture manufactured prior to 1950 (you may be required to provide the Trading Standards Office with evidence of the manufactured date or a statement of age given by an appropriately experienced assessor)
- bed clothes (including duvets).

Upholstered furnishing must have fire resistant filling and pass the 'match' and 'cigarette' test to be compliant with the Regulations. They must also have affixed to them the appropriate manufacturer's label (see Figure 4). Beds and mattresses do not need to have permanent labels attached but must meet British Standard BS7177 (a label attached at purchase should confirm this).

Labels can get damaged or become loose or worn over time and, as these are your main evidence proving compliance, you should record details at the point of purchase. Register:

- the date of purchase
- where purchased
- the manufacturer
- model and reference numbers
- a verbatim transcript of what is displayed on any label(s).

Pin to this record your purchase receipt and a photograph of the item of furnishing with the permanent label(s) clearly visible. Keep these in a safe place for future reference. The Department of Trade and Industry has produced a useful free Guide to the Furniture and Furnishings (Fire) (Safety) Regulations which includes a pictorial reference of all mandatory labels required. Contact the Department's publications unit on 0870 1502 500 or visit **www.dti.gov.uk/access/furniture/contents.htm** on-line. A copy of the full Regulations can be ordered from the HMSO or at **www.hmso.gov.uk** (enter Furniture and Furnishings into the search facility).

FIRE SAFETY LEGISLATION
The relevant legislation includes:

- The General Product Safety Regulations 1994
- The Housing (Management of Houses in Multiple Occupation) Regulations 1990
- Fire Precautions Act 1971 (S.10)
- Housing Acts 1980 and 1985
- The Consumer Protection Act 1987

Some of these Acts and Regulations apply only to HiMO landlords and/or commercial landlords who let property as part of a business. Current legislation does, however, provide various powers to local authorities, trading standards officers, environmental health officers, the fire service, and/or other agencies, to inspect properties reported or suspected to be unsafe. All landlords should examine their property and the appliances and furnishings therein to ensure they meet the required standards. In particular:

◆ Communal hallways and staircases should be free of any obstructions which may inhibit a quick exit during a fire. Carpet laid to stair-steps must be secure with no threadbare patches that could cause someone to trip or fall.

◆ If extinguishers and other fire-fighting equipment are provided, they should be in good working order and meet the required British Standard. User instructions should be easy to read and the equipment should be tested according to the manufacturer's guide or appropriate legislation, depending on the type of property being let (consult your local environmental health department).

◆ Properties considered to be a HiMO (see Chapter 1) must conform to the fire-safety standards enforced by the local authority.

◆ Consider the fire escape route and assess whether it could be improved.

◆ If you are considering making significant changes to the dwelling, be certain to check with the local authority planning department/building control before proceeding, to ensure compliance with building and fire safety regulations.

◆ Building Regulations require all properties built after June 1992 to have a mains powered inter-connected smoke-alarm system installed. Landlords of older properties should consider providing at least a battery-operated smoke-detector as it will add considerably to the safety of their tenants. Alarms should be fitted in an effective location and supplied with new batteries at the start of each tenancy. Testing and maintenance should be specified within the tenancy agreement, so that all are clearly aware of who is responsible.

HEALTH AND SAFETY ISSUES

By supplying accommodation, furnishings, appliances and equipment to tenants, you are required by law to observe the health and safety issues that may affect them. This involves you conducting a risk-assessment and satisfying yourself that the property and its contents are safe. The following represent some of the more significant areas of concern.

Asbestos

Does the property contain asbestos? Older properties were often built using asbestos for sewerage pipes, drainage, roofing and to line walls. Removal is usually required unless it is in good order and safely encapsulated. Consult the local environmental health department for further advice.

Damp and mould

High levels of humidity, combined with inadequate ventilation, is a serious health hazard for occupiers. Any condensation or dampness should be investigated and the cause remedied.

Ventilation

Unventilated bathrooms and kitchens should have a ceiling or wall-mounted extractor fan. Opening windows should be tested after any painting has been undertaken.

Sharp objects

Examine the property for protruding nails, broken or cracked glass and any splintered timbers that may cause injury. Repair or replace as necessary before the property is occupied.

Sanitation

Basins, sinks, baths, shower bases, toilet bowls and cisterns should be free of defects. Any that are cracked or damaged should be replaced.

Safety rails

The bannister rails leading up a staircase must be securely fixed, as should bath-handles (where fitted), any rails leading down into a cellar, and any gallery or balcony railings.

Carpets

Floor coverings should always be in a good condition with no threadbare, loose or worn areas that could cause an accident. It is impossible for all eventualities to be considered and the law recognises that tenants must employ a degree of commonsense when occupying a property. However, landlords have a **duty of care** to their tenants and must take all necessary precautions to supply safe accommodation, free of any obvious hazard.

SUMMARY

- As a landlord letting property in England and Wales, you must comply with the laws and regulations affecting you and your property.

- Arrange for both electrical and gas safety inspections to be conducted in accordance with the appropriate legislation and before occupation of the property by tenants.

- Inspect all furnishings and confirm that they comply with the Furniture and Furnishings (Fire) (Safety) Regulations 1988 (as amended in 1989 and 1993). Resist the temptation to buy second-hand goods if compliance is suspect or cannot be proved.

- Be aware of the fire-safety laws affecting your property and, if in any doubt about compliance, consult the environmental health officer of the local authority.

- Inspect for any potentially hazardous installations, fittings, equipment or appliances that could lead to injury or ill-health. Repair or replace anything that is damaged, cracked, loose or otherwise defective.

4

Preparing the Property for Tenants

In this chapter:

- ◆ decoration
- ◆ furnished or unfurnished?
- ◆ insurance
- ◆ creating an introductory pack
- ◆ manuals, keys and code numbers.

Good preparation from the start will mean fewer problems later. These are the final tasks you need to perform before introducing viewers to the dwelling.

DECORATION

No matter how careful your tenant is, there will always be minor damage to décor. Use materials that are easily renewed; paint is the obvious first choice as it is inexpensive and quick to apply. As a general guide consider the following:

- ◆ Don't use strong exotic colours; not all potential tenants will find them attractive. Instead, use matt emulsion off-white shades or magnolia for all walls. This creates an illusion of space and will appeal to most people.

- ◆ Retain a small amount of paint to repair minor scuff marks caused during tenancy.

- Paint all skirtings, timber window frames and sills, doors and door frames with white gloss.

- Paint ceilings with a proprietary matt white emulsion.

FURNISHED OR UNFURNISHED?

Local demand will be a major influence in deciding whether to furnish your property. Where there is a highly mobile tenant population, for example within large inner city areas, it is often better to offer a furnished dwelling. This group move frequently and usually do not want the added cost and inconvenience of transporting their possessions.

Conversely, in some rural areas with a less mobile population and where tenancy terms are longer, it can be worth offering a property unfurnished. These tenants often want to establish a home and will wish to fill it with possessions of their own choice and style.

Consider the following when making your decision.

The disadvantages of supplying furnished

- The landlord is liable for the repair or replacement of any furniture, appliances and equipment supplied during the tenancy (subject to the tenancy agreement wording and statutory rights of the tenant).

- Any furniture, appliances and equipment must be supplied in a good and safe condition and some items must be professionally inspected (see Chapter 3).

- Your choice of furnishings may discourage some would-be tenants whose personal preference and style may differ.

◆ The cost of supplying, maintaining and replacing furnishings may not be offset by a higher rent, particularly with larger properties where a vast array of items will be required.

◆ Between tenancies, furnishings and equipment will be vulnerable to theft or accidental damage. Landlords should consider arranging suitable insurance cover to protect them.

◆ There is currently no council tax exemption for landlords of vacant furnished dwellings (unless substantial major repairs or structural work are required). The 'empty' rate therefore applies (normally 50% of the full rate). Unfurnished and unoccupied dwellings are currently exempt from council tax for the first six months (changes are being proposed which may remove this concession).

◆ Creating an inventory of furnishings, appliances and equipment at the start of tenancy, and checking it again at the end, takes time. The more items there are on the inventory, the longer it will take. If an inventory clerk is employed, the cost will be an additional expense deducted from rental income.

The advantages of supplying furnished
◆ A furnished dwelling can appear more homely and be more appealing to would-be tenants. This may result in faster occupation rates and reduced void periods.

◆ Less damage will be caused to walls and doors because tenants will not have to move large items in and out.

◆ Supplying furnishings can be expensive to people with restricted finance. Although the rent may be a fraction higher in comparison to an unfurnished dwelling, it may seem advantageous to the tenant to have them provided, with the cost extended over a long period.

♦ The Inland Revenue provide landlords of furnished properties with an allowance against tax currently at 10% of the rent to cover depreciation, repair and replacement.

If, after careful consideration, you decide to let your property furnished, only provide the essentials. Remember you are not supplying a holiday letting – so don't provide small, inconsequential items such as cutlery, pictures, pots and pans, ornaments and linen. Most tenants will wish to acquire these themselves to create a home characterised by their own personality and taste.

Don't supply hi-tech equipment such as a video, television or hi-fi unit. These are vulnerable items if left in an unoccupied property. They are also expensive to repair or replace. Note also that landlords who provide a television are liable for the licence fee during empty periods.

INSURANCE

Although you may already have either buildings and/or contents insurance for your property, there are good reasons for carefully assessing the protection they provide. Many policies offer no cover for tenanted properties, whilst others do not offer sufficient protection. Some only do so for certain types of tenant. Read the small print thoroughly and assess their value based on the letting plans you have made. Consider in each case whether the policy includes:

♦ Loss of rent if the property becomes uninhabitable.

- The expense of providing suitable alternative accommodation if the tenant has to temporarily move out for repairs and where the cost is greater than the rent currently being paid.

- Cover regardless of the tenant type (some policies prohibit students and/or tenants in receipt of benefit).

- Cover during empty periods.

- Accidental damage to the landlord's possessions (there is no statutory requirement to insure the tenant's possessions, though in some circumstances they may have grounds to seek compensation).

- Public liability cover where a tenant, their guest or other visitor injures themselves due to a fault in the building or any supplied furniture or equipment.

- Legal expenses cover should a tenant decide to take court proceedings against you.

Some insurance policies are specifically designed for let-property. Although many are only available through letting agents, some landlords' associations also provide them, and the cost of membership can often be fully reimbursed through reduced insurance premiums. Check *Yellow Pages* or consult your local authority for any groups that have been established in your local area. Alternatively, if you have internet access, send me an e-mail *(tony_booth@btopenworld.com)* and I will reply in due course with any available information pertinent to where you live. To obtain on-line landlords' insurance quotes, visit **www.insurancewide.com** where you will also find additional information on this subject.

CREATING AN INTRODUCTORY PACK

There is no legal obligation to provide tenants with an introductory pack, but it *is* advisable. Anything that assists them to enjoy the property and its location may encourage a renewal of tenancy. In addition, providing instructions may prevent accidental damage occurring as tenants try to operate equipment using guesswork alone. A comprehensive pack might include:

◆ Instructions and/or operation manuals for all supplied equipment, appliances, systems and installations.

◆ Information about security matters including contact details for the local police and any Neighbourhood Watch scheme.

◆ Your contact details, including any out-of-hours emergency telephone number.

◆ A local map.

◆ Bus and train timetables.

◆ Guide notes for cleaning the oven, freezer, curtains and carpets.

◆ Emergency telephone numbers for gas, water and electricity.

◆ Information on local schools, libraries, leisure facilities, good bars and recommended restaurants, the nearest park, train station, bus stop, etc.

◆ Information about where the mains water stop-tap is located.

◆ Information about where the electricity and gas meters are located together with guide notes on how to turn off each supply.

◆ Space for copies of the tenancy agreement, inventory and any letters you send to the tenants.

The pack can be used for each subsequent tenancy, expanding with additional information as required. A wallet-file with A4 document pockets will help keep everything organised.

MANUALS, KEYS AND CODE NUMBERS

Manuals

Legislation demands that landlords supply instruction manuals or written guide notes for certain types of equipment, appliances, installations and systems. It is good practice to give tenants a *full* range of instructions for all the goods provided. Unfortunately, tenants have a habit of losing these documents, so give copies and keep the originals safe.

Copy keys

Landlords should have one set of keys for each tenant plus two sets for themselves. This may seem excessive, but if a tenant loses their keys and demands a new set on Sunday afternoon, obtaining new copies from the master set could prove difficult. Always imagine the worst-case scenario...and then have a plan to deal with it!

You will need copies of *all* keys, not just those for the main entrance door. This might include a garage, garden shed, conservatory, patio doors, window locks, garden gate, any padlocks supplied, mail-box or outhouse.

Code numbers

Some alarm systems, communal entrance doors and security gates use a code number. It is imperative that your tenants are issued with these codes but a security risk might arise when the tenant finally vacates. To combat this, never supply an instruction manual that includes a procedure for changing the code. Instead, obliterate this section when copying the manual so that you alone have access to this process. When the tenant vacates, the code can be altered, and security will be maintained.

SUMMARY

◆ Use paint, not wallpaper, when decorating as it is easier to maintain and renew.

◆ Decide whether or not to furnish your property according to the local demand. Supply only essential and bulky items, and of a quality and style appropriate for the type of tenant.

◆ Check that existing insurance policies adequately protect you and your property. Confirm that letting is not prohibited. Assess the value of changing your policies to ones specifically designed for landlords.

◆ Create an introductory pack for your tenants and include copies of all manuals and instructions for equipment, appliances and systems.

◆ Ensure you have enough copy keys.

◆ Maintain security when issuing tenants with code numbers.

5

Creating an Inventory

In this chapter:

- identifying the inspection areas
- using a reference guide
- undertaking the inspection
- creating the inventory
- the value of photographs
- inventory clerks
- template forms.

An entire chapter has been dedicated to this subject...and with good reason! The **inventory** of furnishings and fittings is one of the most important documents a landlord can create, yet so few do it properly. Many believe it is sufficient to list items haphazardly with little or no regard to accurate identification, description or condition. It is little wonder that these same landlords suffer the consequences of a protracted dispute at the end of tenancy, when damage is found and they claim compensation from the tenant's deposit.

The inventory is the landlord's only evidence of how the property was provided at the outset. It should accurately describe, in fine detail, everything within it. Should a dispute have to be settled in court, this document will need to paint a tangible picture to people who have not seen the accommodation, so that a judgement can be made. Time and care should be taken *now* to produce a comprehensive and faithful report that can be relied upon later, should the need arise.

IDENTIFYING THE INSPECTION AREAS

Start by walking through and around the property, listing every space within it. This will provide the headings you will use later to catalogue items in the spaces. Ensure these 'titles' are descriptive of the rooms to which they relate. Rather than use *'Bedroom No 1'*, you might call it *'Largest Bedroom to Front Elevation'*, which more accurately identifies its location within the dwelling. Include any loft-space or cellar, garden areas, shed, greenhouse, garage, staircase, landing, hallway, hot-water tank cupboard, storage cupboard, conservatory, vestibule, balcony, roof-terrace or patio. Now take as many sheets of paper as required and write one heading at the top of each.

Only include those areas pertinent to the tenancy. Exclusive possession cannot be granted to regions such as communal gardens or shared entrances and stairwells. These should therefore be excluded from the inventory.

USING A REFERENCE GUIDE

Before conducting an inspection, it is useful to have a reference to remind you of the various observations you need to make as you progress through each space within and around the property. On a separate sheet of paper, write the following:

1. **Colour**. Be descriptive. *'Post-box red'* is clearer than *'red'* alone.

2. **Material**. Cotton, wood, glass, metal, ceramic, etc. Be specific, but only if you are certain; use *'bronze figurine'* only if you are certain the material is bronze. An alternative might be *'dark metal figurine'*.

3. **Manufacturer**. Who produced it? Most goods are labelled or stamped with the manufacturer's name.

4. **Model/serial number or name**. As 3 above.

5. **Size**. Be as precise as possible. Use a ruler or tape measure.

6. **Shape**. Is it square, oval, spherical, box, etc?

7. **Labels**. This is to remind you to check the existence of a compliance label on furnishings requiring one (see Chapter 3). Make a note identifying the location of any fixed labels, for example *'under seat cushion'*.

8. **Condition**. Look for cracks, stains, blemishes, marks, scratches, scuffs, erosion, fading or wearing. Carefully detail the degree and location of any damage. Decide whether the item is in **good** (as new), **fair** or **poor** condition.

9. **Tested**. What date was the item last tested (electrical and/ or gas appliances, equipment, installations and systems)? Refer to the engineer's report.

UNDERTAKING THE INSPECTION
You will need:

- the reference guide
- headed sheets

- tape measure
- step-ladders for access into the loft, if necessary.

Start at the uppermost part of the property. It is important that nothing is missed from the inventory so be logical in your approach. Examine the ceiling and any light fittings. Then work down each wall looking at the windows, any curtains or blinds, pictures, shelving and wall-heaters; end with the floor-covering and anything standing on it. Remember to include doors and skirtings, power-sockets, wall-coverings, and any items stored in cupboards.

Once the interior has been fully recorded, move outside (if appropriate) and examine the entrance doors, any porch, garden areas, sheds, greenhouse, garage, dividing wall or fence.

CREATING THE INVENTORY

Figure 5 is an example of how to compile the information into a single report. It describes part of one room only; it is not the entire inventory. Use this as a template for each room or space in your property, giving regard to any necessary alterations according to the design, size and quality of the dwelling and items it contains. At the top of each page write the address of the dwelling and the page number. At the bottom write *'Tenant(s) Signature(s)'* (tenants should always sign every page to prove they have seen them).

The bulk of the inventory is now complete. There are a few additions to be made, including a front page title:

603 LAPWING COURT,
JERRADINE WAY
MANCHESTER
M49 8HRF.

(KITCHEN)

QTY.	ITEM	DESCRIPTION	TENANT COMMENTS
	CEILING	WHITE PAINTED PLASTER IN GOOD CONDITION	
	WALLS	MAGNOLIA EMULSION PAINTED PLASTER IN A GOOD CONDITION	
	WINDOWS	x 2 UPVC DOUBLE GLAZED UNITS WITH CLEAR PANES IN GOOD CONDITION	
	FLOOR	VINYL TILED IN A PLAIN CREAM COLOUR GOOD CONDITION	
	TIMBERS INCLUDING DOOR, SKIRTINGS AND DOOR FRAME	PAINTED WHITE GLOSS, ALL IN A GOOD CONDITION	
1	CEILING MOUNTED FLORESCENT LIGHT FITTING	WITH DIFFUSER AND WORKING TUBE	
	RANGE OF FITTED MATCHING WALL AND BASE UNITS	WITH LIGHT NATURAL TIMBER DOORS AND DRAWER FRONTS WITH POLISHED METAL HANDLES ALL IN GOOD CONDITION	
	MOTTLED CREAM LAMINATE WORKTOPS	SCRATCH MARKS TO SURFACE NEAR SINK	
1	ZANUSSI AUTO WASHING MACHINE, PLUMBED IN MODEL AQUACYCLE	SERIAL No ZN335603F CLEAN CONDITION LAST SAFETY TEST UNDERTAKEN 23 FEB 2003	
1	WALL MOUNTED ELECTRIC STORAGE HEATER	SCRATCH TO PAINTED FRONT SURFACE LAST SAFETY TEST UNDERTAKEN ON 23 FEB 2003	
4	TIMBER FRAMED CHAIRS WITH UPHOLSTERED SEATS	BLUE AND WHITE STRIPE FABRIC. FIRE SAFETY COMPLIANCE LABELS ATTACHED UNDER EACH SEAT. ONE SEAT STAINED.	

TENANT(S) SIGNATURE(S) ....

Fig. 5. Example page from an inventory.

INVENTORY and SCHEDULE OF CONDITION
of Furnishings and Fixtures for
(address of property to be tenanted)

The next page details *'Notes for the Tenant'*. These might include the following (but confirm that they are compatible with the wording of terms in the tenancy agreement, otherwise a conflict may arise):

◆ This inventory is an accurate description of items supplied with this property. It is agreed all items are in a good condition unless otherwise stated.

◆ The property is in a clean condition. Charges will be incurred by the tenant if, at the end of the tenancy, the property is returned in an inferior condition.

◆ All items of furnishing/appliances must be in their original location and position prior to vacating the property.

◆ Garden areas (if appropriate) must be returned at the end of tenancy in the same neat and well-maintained state.

◆ Carpets, curtains and other soft furnishings must be returned at the end of tenancy in the same condition as detailed in this inventory. There will be a charge for any stains, marks or other damage caused, according to the degree of reinstatement required.

◆ Fair wear and tear will be taken into consideration. However, you will be charged for damage to wallpaper, walls, doors, ceilings, and any other surface found punctured, scratched or otherwise damaged by nails, pins, hooks, screws, drills, knives or any other object.

◆ Breakages or damage must be reported and resolved at the time of occurrence and in a manner and quality commensurate with the item supplied.

◆ There must be no work, alteration or repair of any kind conducted to the structure of the property or to anything contained within it or to the grounds, unless the landlord's written authority has been received.

◆ Tenants must not, under any circumstances, change or add to any locking device within the property. All keys must be returned at the end of tenancy. If access cannot be gained by the landlord due to changed locks or missing keys, the tenant will be charged for any work or materials required.

The last page of the inventory should include any items not stored in any specific room. These might include:

◆ Appliance manuals – listed individually.
◆ Other instructions or care notices.
◆ The information pack.
◆ Keys – detail the number and type and the doors or windows they open.

This page should also include a space at the bottom for the tenant's name, his signature, the landlord's signature, the date, and a disclaiming statement similar to the following:

This inventory provides a detailed and fair account of the items provided to the tenant(s) on [date] and the condition of these items and of the décor, gardens (if any), fabrics, timbers, painted surfaces, and all other parts and objects forming the whole of the tenanted premises. The writer is not a surveyor, engineer or structural surveyor; nor is he an expert in materials, timbers, fabrics, colours, antiques, etc. Descriptions given are done so in good faith and with relevance only to their existence and perceived condition.

Two identical copies of the inventory will be required for 'check-in' (see Chapter 9).

Avoid the use of abbreviations

Do not use abbreviations unless a clear explanation of their meaning is given. Even the common use of 'N/A' for not applicable or 'WC' for water closet can lead to misinterpretation.

THE VALUE OF PHOTOGRAPHS

Photographic evidence of the condition of the property and its contents is an advantage. It will support the written inventory and graphically depict elements to any third party. When obtaining photographs:

- Take at least two or three wide shots in each room or area, paying particular attention to wall-coverings, carpets and the flat surfaces of tables.

- Capture specific items that may be prone to damage or which are of particular concern.

- Obtain evidence of a clean oven, hob, fridge, kitchen cupboards, shower or bath.

- If gardens are in a neat and well-maintained state, take a few photographs of the exterior.

◆ Use a camera that records the date on photographs. Alternatively, write the date pictures are taken on the reverse of photographs later.

◆ Use a video camera in preference, or in addition, to producing stills.

INVENTORY CLERKS

There are firms of inventory clerks who offer services to landlords for a fee. The main benefit is that a professional inventory is more likely to be considered impartial by all parties involved. This can be important if a dispute over dilapidations arises at the end of the tenancy. An experienced inventory clerk will differentiate fairly between wear and tear and damage; whereas a landlord could be biased in making judgement.

To locate a firm in your area consult *Yellow Pages* or telephone the *Association of Independent Inventory Clerks* on 01483 757557.

TEMPLATE FORMS

Inventory forms can be ordered at **http://kit.freelet.co.uk** for £4 per pack. These have not been examined by the author of this book and therefore no comment about quality or suitability can be given. A free version of an inventory form is also available online at **www.landlordzone.co.uk**

SUMMARY

◆ Identify the property's interior and exterior spaces and convert them into headings for the inventory.

◆ Create a reference of inspection elements.

- Undertake thorough scrutiny of the property contents and assess the condition of each item. Record full details including any identification model or serial numbers, manufacturer (if known), colour, shape and size.

- Record when electrical and gas appliances/fittings were last inspected for safety.

- Identify all fire safety labels and record where they are located if affixed to upholstered items.

- Create two copies of the inventory document. Ensure there is enough space for tenants to write their comments on the day of entry.

- Take photographs of the property interior and exterior.

- Consider employing an inventory clerk.

6

Finding Suitable Tenants

In this chapter:

- ◆ advertising the property
- ◆ the value of 'to let' boards
- ◆ accepting pets and young children
- ◆ contacting local employers
- ◆ alternative tenant sources
- ◆ creating an application form
- ◆ showing the property
- ◆ interviewing potential tenants.

Finding a tenant is not difficult, but finding the *right* tenant is an entirely different matter. This chapter deals only with the initial part of this process; the next chapter looks at verifying the proposed tenant's identity and background.

ADVERTISING THE PROPERTY
Traditional advertising in local newspapers can produce a horde of enquiries, but can be expensive and not always successful. For the best results:

- ◆ Examine other landlords' advertisements and make your rent competitive, given the size and quality of accommodation and its location.

- Identify which editions of a daily newspaper are popular with those searching for let property.

- Use the three best assets of the dwelling in the first sentence of your advert.

- Plan ahead. Be available to answer calls once the advert is published. Avoid using an answer-machine as some callers will not leave a message.

- Be prepared. When calls are expected, have a couple of pens available (in case one fails), a notepad, calendar or diary for viewing appointments, and a list of suitable questions. Double-check that you have written down the enquirer's name, address and contact number accurately.

THE VALUE OF 'TO LET' BOARDS

'To let' boards are of paramount importance, particularly where there are other dwellings to rent in the same area. Letting agents will be advertising these other properties and will attract and deliver interested potential tenants right to your doorstep. A 'to let' board shows that you also have accommodation available and people will contact you for more information. Boards also inform neighbours who, in turn, will tell their friends, colleagues and relatives about the property. Do not underestimate the power of word-of-mouth.

Boards can be self-made or created professionally. Once tenants have been found, the board should be stored away so it can be used again when the property becomes vacant.

ACCEPTING PETS AND YOUNG CHILDREN

It is useful to decide whether or not you intend to accept tenancy applications from people with pets or young children. Determining this in advance greatly reduces the number of disappointed applicants but, by being selective, you will receive less enquiries.

Until the Office of Fair Trading (OFT) released its guidance notes on *Unfair Terms in Tenancy Agreements* in 2001 (which relate to the *Unfair Terms in Consumer Contracts Regulations 1999*), it **was** generally accepted that private sector landlords could prohibit the keeping of *all* pet animals through a clause in the tenancy agreement. This is no longer safe because the OFT considers it unfair when such a broad term prevents the tenant from keeping, for example, a goldfish. The guidance notes suggest that prohibiting a specific type of pet *that might harm the property or be a nuisance to other residents* would be more appropriate and less likely to meet the same objection.

However, once tenants are in occupation, it is unlikely that a landlord will regain possession through the courts simply because tenants have young children or are keeping pet animals. There would have to be considerable evidence of a nuisance to neighbours or excessive damage for there to be even a remote chance of success. Taking this into account, landlords should reject inappropriate tenants at the application stage.

CONTACTING LOCAL EMPLOYERS

Research shows that 75% of people who drive to work live within two miles of their place of employment. The best way of targeting this group is to identify the major employing companies in the area and visit each one in person. Take with you a single page which describes the accommodation, the rent and your contact particulars. Make it more eye-catching by including a photograph. In addition:

♦ Take drawing-pins so that a copy can be attached to any staff notice board.

♦ Ask whether there is a company newsletter you can advertise in.

♦ Enquire about an *intranet* service where you can post your property details. An intranet is like the internet, but restricted to a company and its employees.

♦ Leave copies of the property details with any personnel or accommodation officer and explain that you would accept an individual tenancy or a company letting.

♦ Follow up your visits with courtesy telephone calls one week later to check for enquiries.

ALTERNATIVE TENANT SOURCES

There are scores of opportunities to advertise properties and find suitable tenants. These are just a few:

♦ Libraries often allow anyone to display information on public notice-boards.

♦ Most supermarkets have notice-boards for their customers to use.

♦ Colleges and universities often have information boards too. It is not only students who need accommodation but lecturers and administration staff as well.

- Hospitals are a good source for tenants. There are ancillary workers, administration staff, doctors and nurses always looking for rented property.

- Do not overlook local schools; teachers and other staff are often searching for homes nearby.

- Airports are also useful, particularly if you can find a notice-board inspected by flight-crew.

- Bus terminals and major railway stations often have hundreds of employees operating in and from them. Find the staff information board and pin details to it.

- If your property is an apartment, post copies of your details under each door in the block. Owners or tenants may have friends, colleagues or relatives looking for similar properties to rent.

- Although you may not wish to employ a managing agent, some letting agents offer a tenant-find-only service. The cost is usually about a month's rent equivalent.

The internet is a valuable source of advertising though success may be hit-and-miss because there are thousands of property related websites, each containing scores of property-to-let details; it must be like finding a needle in a haystack for tenants searching for a specific type of accommodation. The more popular websites charge a fee for advertising, but currently all of the following offer it free:

www.accommodation.com   www.privateagent.co.uk
www.ad-mart.co.uk   www.propertydatabase.co.uk
www.easylet.org.uk   www.propertylocator.co.uk
www.estateagent.co.uk   www.rentamatic.co.uk

www.flats-for-rent.com	www.residentialrentals.co.uk
www.homes2rent.net	www.simplyrent.co.uk
www.interlettings.com	www.thehouseexchange.co.uk
www.letbynet.com	www.torent.co.uk
www.letsdirect.co.uk	www.ukpropertymove.co.uk
www.loot.com	

To advertise on five of the more popular UK rented property websites, with an audience of over 300,000 visitors a week, go to **www.froglet.com** For £15 you can have unlimited advertising space and upload up to five photographs (advert remains active for one month).

CREATING AN APPLICATION FORM

It is important to provide all potential tenants with an application form because:

- it ensures the collection of accurate personal data so that suitability can be properly assessed

- it provides the required information for referencing purposes

- it confirms the applicant's intention to proceed

- and it grants the landlord the authority to seek additional data from third parties (such as banks and employers).

Even more importantly:

- it can provide the landlord with a means of regaining possession through the courts using **Ground 17**. This relates to a tenancy based on information supplied by an applicant which is later found to be false or misleading.

The best application form is one devised to meet your own particular needs and circumstances. However, there are certain elements that are common to all landlords and all properties. These include:

1. The applicant's full name.

2. The applicant's full postal address, post-code and occupancy status (owner-occupier, tenant, lodger, parent's home, etc). Existing tenants should supply their landlord's contact details.

3. The applicant's prior address (if less than five years at the one above). As in 2 above, the status of residency should be identified.

4. The applicant's date of birth.

5. The full name(s) and age(s) of any person(s) intending to live with the applicant at the property. *Note*: a separate application form should be completed by each person over 18 proposing to be a joint-tenant, i.e. who intend paying rent and/or residing as a co-tenant.

6. The relationship of all named at 5 above to the applicant, for example, husband, wife, partner, parent, guardian, colleague, friend.

7. Occupation details including whether full-time, part-time or self-employed. The period with the current employer, salary (excluding bonuses, commissions and over-time), position held, and the full name, address and telephone number of the employer.

8. If not employed, the funds from which rent will be paid. This may be a pension, housing benefit, capital in bank, etc.

9. Details of previous or existing criminal convictions (Rehabilitation of Offenders Act) or County Court Judgements (CCJs). If none, it is important the applicant states so in writing.

10. Whether a pet will be kept in the dwelling and, if so, the type of pet.

11. Whether the applicant is a smoker.

12. Bank details including the name of the account (important with joint accounts if the second account holder needs to give permission for information to be released), the account number, sort-code, and name and address of the bank.

13. Accountant's details (if self-employed) plus a copy of the last year's annual accounts.

14. Whether the applicant has ever been declared bankrupt.

15. Character reference details.

16. The applicant's National Insurance number.

17. The name, address and relationship to any intended guarantor. If there is none arranged, then the applicant should confirm this.

18. Proof of identification. It is important to confirm the person applying for tenancy is the same person who views the property. Ask for copies of the applicant's passport *and* driving-licence *or* birth-certificate.

There should be a space for a signature on each page of the form. The final section should include a statement as follows (providing it is compatible with the wording of the tenancy agreement and does not create any confusion or conflict):

This application is for a residential Assured Shorthold tenancy at (address) for a period of (fixed term). I understand the rent payable will be £(amount) per month by bank standing-order. I understand and accept that I will be liable for payment of the council tax, all gas and electricity charges, water and sewerage charges, any telephone service, cable and satellite service charges and the television licence, during the period of tenancy. I will be responsible for opening accounts with service providers at the start of tenancy and for closing accounts and making final balance payments at the end of tenancy.

Upon entry to the property I will pay one month's rent in advance together with a security deposit of £(amount) in cash or bank-draft. The security deposit will be retained by the landlord in lieu of any damage, breakages, cleaning, unpaid accounts and/or keys and locks needing replacement (other than normal fair wear and tear). I understand that the deposit cannot be used for rent payment during the tenancy.

I confirm that the information provided in this application is correct and accurate and I understand that applying for a tenancy does not create a tenancy agreement or contract.

I hereby authorise the landlord (or his agent) to release copies of this application to third parties, seek references and conduct credit and other personal and/or financial checks as required, within the confines of the Data Protection Act 1988.

This application is subject to contract and dependent upon the landlord's approval before presentation of a tenancy agreement will be considered. A tenancy will not be created until all applicants have signed a tenancy agreement.

Directly below the statement leave a space for the applicant's full name and signature and the date.

There are several versions of tenancy application forms freely available on the internet. One of the best can be found at **www.landlordzone.co.uk**

Before devising and issuing an application form to would-be tenants, read Chapter 7. There are important documents which need to be attached to it and circumstances regarding references which could affect the style of form created.

SHOWING THE PROPERTY

When undertaking viewings:

- Record full details of the people you meet including their full name, address and telephone number.

- Prepare a brief description of the accommodation, deposit and rent, which can be handed to viewers.

- Be aware of personal security issues. If undertaking the viewing on your own, inform a friend or relative of the appointment and arrange to telephone them at an agreed time afterwards.

- Maintain property security. Do not explain the operation of alarm systems or locking devices.

◆ Once the appointment is over, record a brief description of the viewers for future reference.

INTERVIEWING POTENTIAL TENANTS

This type of interview can be undertaken without the candidate ever knowing it. It is not a formal interview, but an assessment conducted surreptitiously, beginning with the first telephone conversation. The caller's main objective is to find out more about the property; yours is to find out more about the caller.

During this initial conversation you should be able to find out whether they intend living on their own or with a joint-tenant; whether married or single; age; telephone manner; whether they work; how long they intend living at the property; where they live now and why they are moving. At the viewing you can observe his punctually, if smartly dressed and polite. Questions can be asked about employment, financial situation and current accommodation.

Once the viewing is over, write a short description and appraisal of the candidate for future reference. Make a note of your instinctive feelings...did you like the individual? Did they seem honest, reliable and trustworthy? Intuition is no substitute for thorough referencing, but it can expose adverse characteristics an individual may be attempting to hide.

SUMMARY

◆ Take every opportunity to market the property to neighbours, colleagues and local employees through traditional advertising, using notice-boards and by erecting a 'to let' board.

- Decide in advance whether to accept tenants with pets or young children, but be aware that it may not always be so easy to prohibit either once a tenancy has begun.

- Take advantage of free advertising on the internet.

- Create a tenant application form pertinent to your own property and requirements.

- Undertake viewings and record important details about potential tenants who show an interest.

7

Tenant Referencing

In this chapter:

- receiving and assessing applications
- discrimination
- employing a reference agency
- obtaining an employment reference
- obtaining a bank reference
- obtaining credit references
- obtaining a landlord's reference
- verifying the home address
- charging costs to the applicant
- guarantors
- company-let referencing.

Appearances can be very misleading. An applicant may seem perfectly suitable at the first meeting. They may be smartly dressed, courteous and respectful. They may appear financially secure and offer to pay the deposit and first month's rent in cash. They may provide credible information that adequately explains their reason for moving.

But this portrayal of the perfect tenant might be a charade. Some of the worst tenants around are adept in the art of deceit, often duping numerous landlords. They will attempt to manoeuvre you into providing them with a tenancy using feigned respect, the lure of cash payments and the promise of a long, trouble-free term of occupancy.

Referencing verifies that the applicant is who they say they are and have the means to pay the rent. Some landlords overlook this essential task and suffer the consequences of housing a bad tenant as a result. Referencing does not offer a cast-iron guarantee against acquiring tenants with adverse qualities, but does improve the odds considerably.

Once a tenant has signed an agreement and is occupying the property, it may be very difficult and costly to deal with any problems they then create. It is always better to reduce the opportunity for difficulties at the outset rather than be forced into dealing with them later.

RECEIVING AND ASSESSING APPLICATIONS

Inspect each application form thoroughly, checking that all questions have been answered and all necessary data supplied. There are various early warning signs which may cause you to be suspicious even before you undertake referencing. These include:

- No bank account details. Either the applicant does not have a bank account (very unusual) or the account is frequently in arrears and they are fearful of you procuring a reference.

- Incomplete data supplied. Either the applicant simply could not be bothered to identify the data or realises providing it could lead to their application being refused.

- Two or more items of information conflict. For example, the date of birth does not reflect the age given or is inconsistent with the age of the person who attended the viewing.

- Failing to provide copies of requested identification documents.

- Applicants who are self-employed but fail to give verifiable evidence of occupation or financial status.

- Applicants who urge you to process their application quickly and offer to pay an early deposit and rent in advance prior to or whilst referencing.

- The application is unsigned or initialled only. The signature should be in the same form as seen on the identification documents.

- One or more application forms missing from the list of individuals wishing to become joint-tenants. Are the cohabiters a stable group?

If there is nothing suspicious about the form received, if you are content with details given and satisfied with the notes you made on the day of viewing, move on to the next question regarding the applicant:

Can they afford the rent?
It is extremely unlikely that you will gain access to the multitude of variables affecting the applicant's financial circumstances at this early stage. Nonetheless, there is a simple but effective calculation to assess suitability. It is one that many reference companies, mortgage lenders and credit agencies adopt as a rough guide:

Monthly rent x 30 = Minimum annual salary

For example, a monthly rent of £550 multiplied by 30 equals £16,500. If the applicant's annual salary is £18,000 then they should be able to afford the rent. However, if their salary is only £15,000 he may find it a strain to meet the rent each month. Although this calculation does not consider specific outgoings or the personal circumstances of each applicant, it is useful as a general guide and I have personally found it to be very effective.

DISCRIMINATION

You must not discriminate on the grounds of:

◆ race and ethnic background
◆ sex
◆ religion
◆ disability.

The Human Rights Act and other anti-discrimination laws prevent landlords from disqualifying tenants under any of the above grounds and severe penalties can be imposed on any that do. You are advised to maintain adequate records showing how decisions about tenancy applications are made and, specifically, why particular applicants are refused.

EMPLOYING A REFERENCE AGENCY

Employing a reference agency is the easiest and often the quickest way to obtain results, but of course there is a cost involved; most charge around £30 for a standard service.

A word of caution: if you intend employing an agency, check the nature of details they will require from applicants. Many have their own style of application form and will insist on this being used for all submissions. Acquire copies in advance to give to your prospective tenants.

Most referencing companies target their services to letting agents rather than to individual private sector landlords. The following are a few who currently offer professional assistance to both:

Experian Tenant Verifier
Talbot House, Talbot Street, Nottingham NG1 5HF
Telephone: 0115 901 6000
E-mail: tenant.verifier@uk.experian.com
Website: **www.tenantverifier.com**

Homelet Tenant Referencing
Homelet House, 30 Thornton Road, Thornton Heath, Surrey CR7 6BA
Telephone: 020 8768 1616
E-mail: ebus@homelet.co.uk
Website: **www.homeletuk.com**

Leaseguard Ltd
Telephone: 01698 368880
E-mail: enquiries@leaseguard.co.uk
Website: **www.leaseguard.co.uk**

LETsure Tenant Assessment
3rd Floor, Rowan House, 70 Buchanan Street, Glasgow G1 3JF

Telephone: 08700 777808
E-mail: info@letsure.co.uk
Website: **www.letsure.co.uk**

Paragon Advance
4–5 The Briars, Waterberry Drive, Waterlooville, Hants PO7 7YH
Telephone: 08700 732235
E-mail: referencing@paragonadvance.com
Website: **www.paragonadvance.com**

The 'do-it-yourself' approach to tenant-referencing involves little more than a few letters and telephone calls and, although it may take a little longer, it will save the cost of a professional service.

OBTAINING AN EMPLOYMENT REFERENCE

Checking an applicant's employment status is essential as some may give false or misleading information, particularly with regard to their length and security of contract and their salary. Figure 6 is an example of the letter you should send to the employer. Attach a copy of the completed application form as it contains an authority for the employer to reply and include a stamped addressed envelope to encourage a faster response.

OBTAINING A BANK REFERENCE

These are the most awkward and frustrating of references you will need to obtain. Awkward because the details supplied by the applicant must be accurate and exact otherwise the bank will not respond with any useful information. Frustrating because, even if the data is correct, the bank is likely to take an

(Your name, address and telephone/fax numbers)

(Name and address of employer)

(Date)

Dear

Ref: (Name of applicant)

The person named above has applied for a residential tenancy from me at £(rent) per month and has given me the authority to contact you for a reference. Please would you respond by answering the following questions and return as soon as possible using the SAE provided.

1. What is his/her annual salary?   £_____

2. Is he/she on a permanent contract with you?   YES ☐ NO ☐

3. How long has he/she been employed by you?   _____

4. Do you consider him/her to be a reliable,
   honest and trustworthy employee?   YES ☐ NO ☐

5. Do you consider his/her salary is sufficient to
   pay the monthly rent of £(rent) given other
   deductions and outgoings?   YES ☐ NO ☐

All information given will be treated in the strictest confidence. Thank you for your time and co-operation in regard to this matter.

PLEASE SIGN HERE   [   ]

YOUR TITLE/POST HELD   _____

Yours sincerely

Fig. 6. Example of an employment reference request.

BANK MANDATE

NAME _____ (Applicant)

ADDRESS _____ (Applicant's home address)

_____

TO: The Manager

_____ (Bank name)

_____ (Address of bank)

_____

_____

(Date)

Dear Sir/Madam,

I/we hereby authorise you to provide information to (landlord's name) of (landlord's postal address) as requested by their letter attached. I/we understand there will be a charge for this and I/we authorise you to deduct the appropriate sum from my/our account held with you, the details of which are:

NAME OF ACCOUNT_____

ACCOUNT NUMBER_____

Please send your reply direct to (landlord's name) at their address as soon as possible.

Yours faithfully,

_____

Account holder's signature(s)

Fig. 7. Example of an applicant's bank mandate.

inordinate amount of time to reply and they rarely give a straightforward answer. They are reluctant to appear disparaging about customers and therefore write in a vague and non-committal manner. This requires a landlord to read between the lines.

A bank might respond by stating they *'are surprised the customer has considered agreeing to a regular expense of this size'.* This implies that the applicant has enough going out of his account already and any additions would strain their resources. Always read a bank reference reply several times and make sure you fully appreciate what is being said.

Be aware that most banks charge a fee for references. Consider obtaining, in advance, a mandate from the applicant allowing the fee to be deducted from their account. This speeds up the process and shows that the applicant has the commitment and confidence to proceed. Figure 7 is an example of a mandate which should be supplied to interested viewers together with the application form. Make sure that this is returned to you duly completed and signed so that a bank reference can be obtained.

Figure 8 is an example of the letter to the bank. Attach the applicant's mandate to the letter. There is no need to provide a reply envelope with this request.

OBTAINING CREDIT REFERENCES

A credit reference is a report compiled by an agency with access to public record data and other private information. This includes details about:

(Your name, address and telephone/fax numbers)

(Name and address of bank)

(Date)

Dear

Ref: (Name of Applicant)

The person named above has applied for a residential tenancy from me at £(rent) per month and has given me the authority to contact you for a reference. Please would you respond by answering the following questions. The applicant has given authority for any charge relating to this reference to be deducted from his account held with you (please see the attached mandate).

1. The applicant intends to pay a deposit of £(deposit) plus rent of £(rent) per month. Do you consider he/she is able to meet these commitments?

    _____

2. Are you aware of any current, impending or future payments that may cause him/her to have difficulty in meeting the regular monthly rent payment?

    _____

3. Are there any additional comments you wish to make relating to the applicant's financial history or circumstances, with regard to his application for a tenancy at the rent stated? If so, please write them here.

    _____

All information given will be treated in the strictest confidence. Thank you for your time and co-operation in regard to this matter.

Yours sincerely

Fig. 8. Example of a bank reference request.

- county court judgements (CCJs)
- credit and hire-purchase history
- electoral roll data
- information on bankruptcy and loan repayments.

The various facts and figures are collated to provide lenders, banks and others with an assessment of an individual's financial history to date. A credit reference enables you to make an objective decision about the level of risk involved in offering a rental agreement to the applicant. Credit references can be obtained from most of the aforementioned companies and charges vary according to the type of report required.

OBTAINING A LANDLORD'S REFERENCE

If the applicant is currently living in rented accommodation, it is important to obtain a reference from his landlord. Use Figure 6 as a template, but substitute the following questions:

- How long is/was the applicant a tenant of yours?
- What is/was the monthly rent being paid?
- Was this rent paid in full and on time each month?
- Were there any periods where the rent was in arrears?
- Is the rent currently in arrears?
- Has the applicant cared properly for the property and its contents?
- Would you accept the applicant as a tenant again?

Some applicants may give false information, possibly because there has been a poor tenant/landlord relationship. The applicant might, for example, give a friend's details instead of their landlord's. One way of checking this is to telephone the landlord acting in the manner of someone searching for rented property. If the response is awkward or confused, you can be fairly certain you are not talking to the applicant's landlord. Seeking a reference would therefore be pointless.

VERIFYING THE HOME ADDRESS

It is important to check that the applicant's given address details are their permanent and registered place of residence. If not, then there will be no record of them having paid utility bills (and therefore no history of good or bad payment) and it will be difficult to trace CCJs without an address by which they can be identified. A reference company will check these facts for you.

It is also possible to undertake this investigation through the internet. Visit **www.192.com** and obtain a password to use their electoral-roll search facility; this service costs £1.50. If the person named is registered at the address given, a map will load as confirmation.

It is also worth asking the applicant to provide the originals (not copies) of two recently paid utility bills (gas, electric, water and/or council tax) displaying their name and address. Check the details against the application form to ensure accuracy.

CHARGING COSTS TO THE APPLICANT

It is perfectly legal for a landlord to charge administrative costs to an applicant. The elements making up this fee might include:

◆ postage
◆ telephone calls

- professional referencing services and credit check
- time given to dealing with the application
- photocopying and/or printing of documents.

The applicant *must* be made fully aware of this charge *before* applying for a tenancy. It must also be made quite clear that the fee is non-refundable, regardless of the outcome of the application. A suitable explanation could be included on the application form together with a request for payment in full. Although many landlords charge an administration fee, it can discourage applicants. Before imposing the levy, consider the level of (tenant) supply and (property) demand at the time.

GUARANTORS

There are various reasons why referencing can fail to provide adequate results. The applicant may not have registered with utility companies, having only recently settled in the country. They may be temporarily working in the UK, but their family and permanent home could be overseas. Or this may be their first application for accommodation away from the parental home. In all of these situations, the would-be tenant's financial history and suitability may be difficult to verify and acquiring a guarantor will therefore be essential.

A **surety guarantor** guarantees the payment of rent and/or other obligations agreed between tenant and landlord. The guarantor becomes legally liable for these contractual commitments if the tenant defaults on payment, causes damage, or breaks some other pertinent condition of tenancy. The guarantor should be referenced in the same manner and to the same degree as an actual tenant. A guarantor agreement is then completed and signed, preferably at the same time as the tenancy agreement. This should always be undertaken face-to-face and with proof of identity to ensure the referenced guarantor is the same person signing the document.

Guarantor agreements can be obtained from most law stationers or alternatively one can be devised for you by a solicitor. Most forms prescribe liability during the initial, fixed term of the tenancy (the contractual period) but *not* for any continuation of the term or renewal of tenancy. It is therefore important to consult with your legal adviser, before completing the form, to ensure suitable clauses are inserted or amendments made that provide for all eventualities arising at the end of the term.

Many landlords and letting-agents accept guarantors routinely because of the nature of their business and rarely report problems in doing so. However, guarantors can frustrate what is already a very complex procedure and, at best, they will create additional administration and a protracted commencement to the tenancy. Novice landlords are best advised to seek an alternative tenant whose reference results are satisfactory, eliminating any need for a guarantor.

COMPANY-LET REFERENCING

If the tenant is to be a company, it is important to undertake full referencing to verify its financial condition and legal status. Professional referencing will ordinarily examine the company's credit worthiness, registered address, limited company status, accounting history and turnover. The agencies listed previously all provide this service.

SUMMARY

- Thoroughly inspect all returned application forms. Check that all sections have been completed and all questions fully answered. Be suspicious of any missing information.

- Before starting the reference process, assess whether the applicant can afford the rent being asked and determine whether they satisfy your tenant criteria.

- Conduct *full* referencing. Consider the advantages of employing an agency to undertake it.

- Decide in advance whether to charge administrative costs.

- Always reference a guarantor to the same degree as the original applicant.

8

The Law of Tenancy

In this chapter:

- ◆ the Housing Acts
- ◆ confirming permission to let
- ◆ tenancy or licence?
- ◆ assured and assured shorthold tenancies
- ◆ unfair tenancy terms
- ◆ obtaining sample tenancy agreements
- ◆ joint tenancies
- ◆ company-let agreements.

The law affecting landlords in England and Wales is vast and complex. A book of this size cannot explain all the regulations involved nor should it be considered a definitive guide to the various individual situations that may be encountered. Both novice and experienced landlords are advised to consult a solicitor specialised in housing law who can counsel on specific problems. Although limited by necessity, this chapter provides a general guide to the legislation and is intended to help instil a greater understanding of what is involved.

THE HOUSING ACTS

These provide the legal framework through which private residential tenancies are created and managed, and contain the definitions, rules and procedures affecting landlords and tenants in England and Wales. The Housing Acts offer statutory protection to both parties and deal with matters including harassment, eviction, tenancy termination, possession rights, rent increases and arrears.

The Housing Act 1988 introduced two types of tenancy – **'assured'** and **'assured shorthold'** – the latter being the most commonly used. Important changes made by the Housing Act 1996 mean that all tenancies created after 28 February 1997 are automatically the assured shorthold type, unless they fail to meet the criteria or the tenant was issued with an appropriate notice stating otherwise (see below). As this book is concerned only with new tenancies, it describes the procedures and regulations dictated by the Acts above only. For older-style tenancies, started prior to 28 February 1997, landlords are advised to seek professional advice. The Housing Acts are only part of the law involved. There is other legislation, such as that affecting furnishings described in Chapter 3, which combine to make up the whole picture.

CONFIRMING PERMISSION TO LET

Before completing the tenancy agreement, you must confirm you have all the necessary documents that legally authorise you to proceed. Where the property to be let has been bought with a **mortgage** you should:

♦ inform the lender *in advance* and *obtain written permission* to create a tenancy in accordance with any contractual obligation to do so; and

♦ incorporate any mandatory demands or restrictions of use, made by the lender, into the tenancy agreement; and

♦ inform the proposed tenant that the property is mortgaged
and explain the implications for them (reference can be
made in the tenancy agreement to an appropriate note for
the purpose of clarity).

Should you fail to meet mortgage payments, the lender may
seek to repossess the property. The tenant is unlikely to have
any legal right to continue occupying it, but could take proceedings against you for being evicted. This may differ where
the lender has recognised the existence of the tenancy and has
agreed to it or where the tenancy was entered into before the
mortgage began. Most lenders insist on prior notice being
issued to tenants (under Grounds 1 and 2 of Schedule 2 of the
Housing Act 1988). It is common practice for such notice to
be included within the body of the tenancy agreement.

Where the property to be let is **leasehold,** you should also
apply for permission from the headlessor. Always obtain such
authority in writing *before* completing the tenancy agreement.

TENANCY OR LICENCE?

Certain conditions must be met in order that a tenancy can be
created. The main criterion is that the tenant has *exclusive* use
of the accommodation. For example, if you are intending to
let a room in your own home or require unrestricted access to
the room then it is likely to be a **licence to occupy**, rather than a
tenancy. Resident landlords cannot usually create an assured
or an assured shorthold tenancy and so different rules and
rights will apply to both the landlord and occupier. It is not
necessary for you to share part of the dwelling with the occupier to be classed as a resident landlord. In some

circumstances, merely living in the same building will be enough! For more information, obtain the free booklet *Letting Rooms in Your Own Home – A Guide for Landlords and Tenants* available from the Department of the Environment, Transport and the Regions (Tel: 0870 1207 405).

ASSURED AND ASSURED SHORTHOLD TENANCIES

This book intends that you create the assured shorthold type of tenancy because it provides the landlord and tenant with mutual benefits. The landlord has a greater degree of security and an easier means of regaining possession at the end of the fixed term. The tenant has a guaranteed period of occupation, providing they maintain rent payments and other tenancy commitments. The descriptions here refer only to tenancies starting after 28 February 1997.

Changes made by the Housing Act 1996 made the creation of an assured shorthold tenancy (AST) very simple and straightforward. In effect, it reversed the prior situation whereby notice had to be served in a prescribed form to create one. It is prudent for us to examine more closely what criteria must exist for an AST to be created and, importantly, what the difference is between the two types.

'Assured' type

This is sometimes referred to as an 'ordinary' or 'full' assured tenancy. The tenant must receive a notice from the landlord stating that it is to be an assured tenancy *before* it begins. If no notice is issued, then it cannot be of this type. Ordinary assured tenants enjoy greater security of tenure. They can occupy the property for an undetermined period and the landlord can only regain possession if they satisfy the courts that certain 'grounds' exist. They have no automatic right to repossess the property just because the tenancy has come to an end. Tenants also have the right to apply for a rent assessment to be conducted and, once assessed, the landlord cannot charge more than the maximum determined.

'Assured shorthold' type

These exist for a fixed period. The tenant does not enjoy indefinite security of tenure. Tenants can apply for a rent assessment during the initial fixed term. Landlords can regain possession of their property at the end of the fixed term or, if the term is less than six months, after six months from the start of tenancy providing appropriate notice is issued to the tenant. If that seems very complicated, don't worry, it will be explained in more detail later. For now it is enough to understand that an AST gives the landlord greater legal powers to obtain possession of the property at the end of the tenancy term. **The tenancy cannot be an assured shorthold if:**

◆ It is a business letting.

◆ It is a holiday let.

◆ It is not the tenant's only or main residence.

◆ The landlord is classed as a resident landlord.

◆ The tenancy began before 15 January 1989.

◆ The tenant is not an individual (this does not exclude joint-tenants).

◆ There is no rent charged or the rent is less than two thirds of the rateable value of the property or is £250 or less a year (£1,000 or less in Greater London).

- The rent charged exceeds £25,000 per year.

- It includes agricultural land of two acres or more or is an agricultural holding.

- The premises are licensed to sell or consume alcohol.

- It is not being let as a separate dwelling.

- The landlord is an educational body, the Crown or a government department, a local authority, housing action trust, or one of several other statutory bodies or a mutual housing association.

- It fails to meet the criteria and definitions laid down in the Housing Act 1988 (as amended by the Housing Act 1996).

UNFAIR TENANCY TERMS

It is no longer safe to write into a tenancy agreement anything that contravenes the OFT's guidelines on unfair tenancy terms. This means that all tenancy agreements must be worded carefully and with due regard to pertinent legislation. To comply, tenancy agreements:

- Must be written without ambiguity and in plain language that tenants are able to understand.

- Must not force unreasonable prohibitions on tenants. For example, a clause that states *'the tenant must not keep inflammable materials on the premises'* prohibits them from storing a box of matches. This is clearly not reasonable and should be better phrased to guard against the storage of materials presenting a genuine fire-hazard.

- Must not force unreasonable obligations on tenants. For example, a clause which states *'the tenant must keep the furnishings clean and dusted at all times'* is unreasonable, as very few people keep their home dust-free at all times.

◆ Should not assume a tenant's comprehension of what is written. For example, the declaration *'I have read and fully understand...'* is unsafe because in practice few tenants read or fully understand all aspects of a tenancy agreement. Declarations might be more acceptable if they begin with *'The tenant **should** read and understand the terms before signing...'*.

◆ Must not exclude the tenant from assigning or subletting. Landlords have a vested interest in preventing their property falling into the hands of unsuitable sub-tenants but, without vetting them, how can they know whether they are unsuitable or not? Global terms are likely to be unacceptable in law, whereas a clause that allows the tenant to sublet in certain circumstances and following a set procedure is more likely to gain favour.

These are just a few of the conditions and examples given in the OFT guide. There are additional **contract** and **consumer** laws that affect the way in which tenancy agreements are worded and the clauses they can legally contain. It is also worth bearing in mind that, whatever is written into an agreement, statute law takes precedence. A tenancy agreement clause cannot override the legal protection afforded to tenants. However, it may frustrate, confuse or invalidate the entire agreement if it has to be submitted to the courts as evidence. Agreements should always be approved by a solicitor experienced in this area of law before being used, regardless of the source.

OBTAINING SAMPLE TENANCY AGREEMENTS

There is a wide range of pre-printed AST agreements available at varying prices. It is important to confirm that any purchased suit the circumstances for which they are intended and that they are up-to-date with current legislation. The following all supply standard forms:

Legal Services Shop
Tel: 020 7239 0104

Stat Plus Group
Tel: 020 8646 5500

Oyez Legal Forms
Tel: 0870 737 7370

The Letting Centre
Tel: 01395 271122

ASTs can also be obtained from the internet at the following sites:

www.easylet.org.uk
www.landlordzone.co.uk
www.legalhelpers.co.uk
www.letonthenet.com

www.compactlaw.co.uk
www.lawpack.co.uk
www.legalshop.co.uk
www.questbrook.co.uk

JOINT TENANCIES

A joint tenancy is one in which the occupants of the same dwelling consist of two or more tenants that are named on the same tenancy agreement. In addition to the warning given about creating a House in Multiple Occupation (see Chapter 1), there are additional problems associated with joint tenancies. These include:

◆ A situation where one of the tenants decides to leave during the term of the tenancy, leaving those remaining to pay the rent or to agree a replacement with the landlord. The former may cause hardship to the tenant(s), resulting in rent arrears; to be legally safe, the latter involves ending the first tenancy and starting a new one, with resulting additional administration and referencing costs. Difficulties can also arise over deposit refunds and who should receive what and when. In addition, during a periodic tenancy, if one tenant issues Notice to Quit then it becomes binding on all other joint tenants, even if they do not agree.

♦ Although joint tenants are usually deemed to be **severally liable** for the rent (i.e., each is equally responsible for the entire sum), in practice tenants share a property because they need to combine incomes to afford the rent. So, if one tenant loses their job or experiences a strain on their resources, the rent may not be paid in full unless the others can (and want) to make up the difference.

♦ Joint tenants who are friends or colleagues, rather than partners, may be cohabiting for the first time and living together may cause unexpected friction. This is particularly likely when the joint tenants are young and have recently moved out of the parental home. The letting may have been requested for a fixed term of six months, but it may fall apart after just one!

When granting a joint tenancy, consider carefully the relationship between the parties and their ability to pay rent independently if things go wrong.

COMPANY-LET AGREEMENTS

Lettings to companies are outside the scope of the Housing Act 1988 and cannot be of the assured or assured shorthold type. This can be advantageous to landlords because these tenants do not enjoy the full statutory protection afforded to individuals. It is, however, important to identify how the accommodation will be used by the company to prevent potential problems arising.

Many do so to accommodate their employees in preference to using a hotel. The employees usually occupy the dwelling as licensees. In these circumstances, when the period of tenancy ends, the occupiers must vacate. However, if the company is allowed to conduct business from the premises, they can apply for protection using the Landlord and Tenant Act 1954; it is therefore important to guard against such activity. The landlord can also prevent the 1954 Act applying by keeping the tenancy term under six months (but not if a series of consecutive tenancies amount to 12 months or more).

Company-let agreements are more difficult to obtain, but some of the previously mentioned suppliers of ASTs also produce sample documents of this type.

SUMMARY

- ◆ Confirm that you have all the necessary written permissions to let from lenders and headlessors.

- ◆ Aim to provide an assured shorthold tenancy as this affords you greater legal protection, but ensure that you and your property meet the criteria contained in the Housing Act first.

- ◆ Obtain a sample agreement and ask your solicitor to ensure it complies with current legislation.

- Be aware of the potential difficulties of a joint tenancy.

- If you intend to provide a company letting, be certain the tenant does not use your property to conduct business and keep the term to a maximum of six months.

9

Starting the Tenancy

In this chapter:

- reserving the property
- deposit and rent payments
- informing utility companies
- postal security
- completing the tenancy agreement
- stamp duty
- check-in
- record-keeping.

Most people assume a tenancy starts on the day an agreement is signed; this is not necessarily true. Neither is it always the case when a tenant takes up occupation or starts paying rent. However, as the day of commencement determines other notable legal dates during and at the end of tenancy, misinterpreting it can lead to security of tenancy being afforded unintentionally to the tenant. This chapter deals with these issues and explains how to prevent problems arising.

RESERVING THE PROPERTY

Tenants occasionally ask landlords to reserve a property. It may be that references have yet to be taken up or they have other commitments causing a delay to immediate occupation, so they may offer to pay a holding fee or both rent and deposit in advance. Landlords need to be extremely cautious in this situation. The lure of money up-front is enticing, but accepting it can create a legally binding arrangement later regretted. The answer is to enter into a pre-tenancy agreement, drafted by your solicitor, which states clearly...

- the amount being paid;

- any non-refundable element or agreed deductions for administration, referencing, keeping the property empty, and other preparatory arrangements;

- the rights of each party to withdraw from proceeding;

- how the sum paid is to be defined if a tenancy is later granted, for example as full or part surety deposit; and

- that the payment is *not* an instalment of rent (because a court might otherwise decide that, even without a written agreement, a tenancy has already begun).

DEPOSIT AND RENT PAYMENTS

Taking a deposit

By concluding all the aspects of tenancy commencement *on the same day* and immediately prior to occupation, there will be less confusion and greater certainty regarding ongoing dates. This involves taking the deposit and first rent-period sums *and* signing the agreement *before* releasing keys. When preparing to accept a deposit, think about:

- **The amount.** Any amount of deposit can be demanded when granting an assured shorthold tenancy. Although one month's rent equivalent is usual, it may be inadequate as some tenants default on paying the last month's rent (leaving the landlord with no security to reimburse the cost of any damage). However, be cautious of accepting more than two months' rent equivalent as it may be construed as a **premium**, giving the tenant an automatic right to **assign** (transfer the tenancy to another person), unless it is specifically precluded by the agreement.

◆ **How it will be paid.** Cheques are not a secure form of payment. Insist on cash or a bank-draft, particularly when taking sums and completing the tenancy on the same day.

◆ **Who owns the money?** It is the tenant's money. The deposit only passes to the landlord *in lieu* of deductions, should any be necessary, at the end of the term and according to provisions contained in the agreement.

◆ **Where it will be kept?** The deposit should ideally be placed in a bank account, separate from the landlord's personal and/or business funds, so it can be clearly identified and not interfered with during the tenancy term. Currently, there is no legal requirement to pay a tenant interest earned on their deposit, but the tenancy agreement should specify whether interest will be earned and, if so, who will receive it.

◆ **Refunding.** We will deal with refunds and dilapidation deductions later in this book. For now, be aware that the tenancy agreement should stipulate that

the deposit less any deductions for unpaid bills, loss, reinstatement, cleaning required, or damage other than fair wear and tear, will be refunded to the tenant's new address within 28 days of the tenancy ending.

This guarantees that you will receive notification of the tenant's next address, which can be fundamental in solving many end-of-tenancy problems!

Setting up rent payments

Rent is paid in advance, therefore a sum covering the first period should be collected in cash or by bank-draft before signing the tenancy agreement. Ongoing rent payments can be arranged by completing a standing-order mandate.

INFORMING UTILITY COMPANIES

Utility companies will only send bills to the tenant *in his or her name* if they are informed about the change of liability. It is therefore important to take meter readings and contact them as soon as tenancy starts (see Figures 9 to 13 for sample letters). The preferred method is to telephone all companies on the commencement date and then confirm immediately in writing, taking copies for the tenant and your files. Where appropriate, contact each of the following:

- local authority council-tax office

- gas supplier

- electricity supplier

- water supplier

- telecommunication company – if the telephone line is in your name, have it disconnected in advance of the tenancy start date to confirm service termination.

POSTAL SECURITY

In time, you may come to trust your tenants. For now, you must consider them as strangers with the skill and desire to commit criminal acts against you. To prevent potential

STANDING ORDER MANDATE

TO:-
(Tenant's Bank Address)

_____ Bank

_____

_____

Post Code _____

PLEASE PAY:-
(Landlord Details)

Bank Name	Branch
Account Number	Sort Code
☐☐☐☐☐☐☐☐	☐☐ — ☐☐ — ☐☐
Beneficiary (Account Name)	

THE SUM OF:-
(Rent Details)

Amount Of Rent	Written In Words
£	

COMMENCING:- | First Payment Date

AND ON THE _____ OF EVERY _____ THEREAFTER UNTIL YOU RECEIVE FURTHER NOTICE FROM ME IN WRITING

DEBITING MY ACCOUNT:-
(Tenant's Account Details)

Account Name	Account Number
	☐☐☐☐☐☐☐☐

SIGNATURE:- _____   **DATE:** _____

NAME IN CAPITALS:- _____

Fig. 9. Sample bank mandate for rent payments.

(Your name, address and telephone/fax numbers)

(Name and address of Council Tax office)

(Date)

Dear

Ref: (Let property address and post code)

Property Reference Number:
(Shown on the last statement received)

I write to inform you that the above property has been let to new tenants from today. The tenant(s) is/are responsible for paying council tax relating to the property. The tenant(s) details are:

Tenant(s) Name(s):

Council Tax Liability Commenced On:

Tenant(s) Prior Address:

Please amend your records accordingly.

Yours sincerely,

Fig. 10. Sample letter for council tax liability.

(Your name, address and telephone/fax numbers)

(Name and address of company supplying gas)

(Date)

Dear

Ref: (Let property address and post code)

Customer Reference Number:
(Shown on the last statement received)

I write to inform you that the above property has been let to new tenants from today. The tenant(s) is/are responsible for paying all charges relating to the supply and consumption of gas at the property. The tenant(s) details are:

Tenant(s) Name(s):

Gas Charges Liability Commenced On:

Tenant(s) Prior Address:

Meter reading taken today:

Please amend your records accordingly.

Yours sincerely,

Fig. 11. Sample letter for gas supply liability.

(Your name, address and telephone/fax numbers)

(Name and address of company supplying electricity)

(Date)

Dear

Ref: (Let property address and post code)

Customer Reference Number:
(Shown on the last statement received)

I write to inform you that the above property has been let to new tenants from today. The tenant(s) is/are responsible for paying all charges relating to the supply and consumption of electricity at the property. The tenant(s) details are:

Tenant(s) Name(s):

**Electricity Charges
Liability Commenced On:**

**Tenant(s) Prior
Address:**

Meter reading(s) taken today:

NORMAL   OFF-PEAK

Please amend your records accordingly.

Yours sincerely,

Fig. 12. Sample letter for electricity supply liability.

(Your name, address and telephone/fax numbers)

(Name and address of the water authority)

(Date)

Dear

Ref: (Let property address and post code)

Reference Number:
(Shown on the last statement received)

I write to inform you that new occupiers have moved into the property above and are responsible for all water and sewerage charges from today. The details are:

Tenant(s) Name(s):

**Water Charges
Liability Commenced On:**

**Tenant(s) Prior
Address:**

Meter Reading Taken Today:
(if property is metered)

Please amend your records accordingly.

Yours sincerely,

Fig. 13. Sample letter for water supply liability.

fraud and/or theft, ensure no mail is delivered to the property containing details of your bank accounts, credit cards, driving licence, or other financial and identification data.

COMPLETING THE TENANCY AGREEMENT

Whilst AST agreements can vary in the number, wording and diversity of terms and conditions forming the bulk of the document, most require similar information to be entered on the first page. This will usually include:

◆ **Property address:** means the let property. Write the full address and post code.

◆ **Landlord:** means you. Write your name in full (and any co-owner).

◆ **Landlord's address:** means the address in England or Wales for tenants to contact you in writing, report damage or for an emergency.

◆ **Tenant:** means those who applied to rent the property from you. This may be an individual, a couple or a group. In each case, write their full name(s).

◆ **Tenant's address:** means the registered prior address(es).

◆ **Term:** means the fixed period of tenancy being granted. For reasons we will discuss later, it is advised you provide a minimum of six months (enter in words).

◆ **Beginning on:** means the first day of tenancy and from when rent becomes due (not necessarily the occupation date). To prevent confusion and possible complications arising later in the tenancy, avoid the 1st, 28th, 29th, 30th and 31st as commencement dates as these can be problematic when calculating the end-of-tenancy and rent-due dates. For example, a six-month tenancy starting on 30 August will expire on 28 February, except during a leap-year when it will be the 29 February.

◆ **Rent:** means the sum covering the period (usually a weekly, monthly or quarterly amount).

◆ **Payable on:** means the date in the month or day of the week that rent becomes due. If a tenancy starts on 6 July then subsequent monthly rent payments fall due on the 6th of each month. Some landlords opt to change the 'rent collection date' to the start or end of the month for convenience, but note that confusion can arise if arrears build up and formal notice needs to be given.

◆ **Deposit:** means the sum received as surety against dilapidations arising at the end of tenancy.

◆ **Date:** means the date the tenancy agreement is signed, which may not necessarily be the same as the date tenancy starts.

Two identical copies of the tenancy agreement will be required and the exact same data must be entered on each one. One copy is **the Agreement**, issued to the tenant(s); the other is **the Counterpart**, retained by the landlord. The significance of these will become clear later in this chapter.

Always use blue or black ink and write in block capitals for clarity. The agreement should confirm that it comprises the details above, the terms and conditions given and the inventory attached. Formal completion (signing) of the agreement *can* be undertaken in advance, but it is best done at the property on the day of tenancy commencement and with all parties present (see 'Check-in' below).

STAMP DUTY

This is a tax applied to legal documents. It is payable on most residential tenancy agreements where the *annual rent exceeds £5,000*. No enforcement rules compel a landlord to stamp the document, but failing to do so can have damaging consequences if they need to submit it to court as evidence when seeking possession or pursuing rent arrears. An agreement that is not stamped cannot be relied on in court. While judges tend to be lenient, it is hardly worth taking a risk given the amounts involved. The duties payable are:

- ◆ **Tenancy with a fixed term of *less* than a year:**
  1. Furnished dwelling and with a rent exceeding £5,000 for the term = £5
  2. Unfurnished dwelling and with a rent exceeding £5,000 per annum = 1% of rent.

- ◆ **Tenancy with a fixed term of one year or more:**
  Furnished or unfurnished dwelling exceeding £5,000 rent per annum = 1% of rent

It is the tenant's responsibility to have the agreement stamped, but few actually do so. The onus therefore falls on the landlord if they wish to confirm admissible competence of the document. Stamp duty can be minimised by granting the tenant a *fixed-term assured shorthold tenancy of six months*. This also provides the landlord with greater legal flexibility under the Housing Act 1988, which we will discuss in more depth later. Your nearest stamp duty office can be found in *Yellow Pages* under 'Government Offices'.

CHECK-IN

Once a date has been agreed for the tenancy to start, it should not be changed unless there are exceptional circumstances. The day before the appointment, telephone the tenant(s) and confirm they are aware:

- of the tenancy commencement date and appointment time;
- that they must have the deposit and rent in cash or bank-draft;
- that it will take approximately one hour to complete the check-in procedure;
- that all applicants must attend the appointment.

Start the tenancy following the procedure below in order:

1. Give both copies of the inventory and ask tenants to verify its accuracy by inspecting the property and its contents. Explain that any additional comments or observations can be entered on the documents in the spaces provided. The tenants should sign and date *both* copies of the inventory. The landlord signs only the **original**, retained by the tenants. The landlord retains the copy that does *not* have his or her signature.

2. Collect the rent and deposit. No receipt is required as the amounts are confirmed as paid in the tenancy agreement. If the rent is to be paid weekly, you must provide a rent book (available from stationers). Obtain the tenants' signatures on the standing-order mandate for ongoing rent payments.

3. Give the tenants both copies of the AST agreement. Ask them to read through it and answer any queries. The

tenants sign and date *one* copy (endorsed as the **counterpart**), retained by the landlord. The landlord signs *one* copy only (**the agreement**), retained by the tenants. This completes the formal process.

4. It is useful to have a witness to the signing of legal documents to help confirm authenticity of the signatures if later disputed. This is not, however, a legal requirement.

5. Supply the tenants with copies of all appliance manuals, instructions and any other documents relating to the property.

6. Explain the operation of intruder alarms, security devices, hot water and heating systems.

7. Explain where emergency shut-off valves, stop-taps and meters are located for gas, electricity and water.

8. Provide copies of letters sent to utility companies.

9. Hand keys over.

10. Advise the tenants of your intention to conduct inspections every three months and that advance written notice will be given when each becomes due. Ensure this is provided for in the tenancy agreement.

11. Explain they should have the tenancy agreement stamped and pay the duty on it (if applicable).

12. Once check-in has finished, have your **counterpart** agreement stamped (costs £5). You can attend the stamp-duty office in person or send the agreement by post (make a copy for safety and be aware it may take 14 days to be returned).

RECORD-KEEPING

Keep a diary specifically for the letting in which important dates can be identified and notes made about telephone conversations with tenants, visits to the property, repair instructions issued to contractors, etc. In addition, full details should be kept separately for rent payments, the issue of notices, electrical and gas safety inspections, and tenancy start and expiry dates. The more information you record, the easier it will be to maintain the tenancy and deal with any problems.

SUMMARY

◆ If tenants wish to reserve your property, consider creating a pre-tenancy agreement and agree any charges should they fail to proceed.

◆ Decide the amount of surety deposit and be aware of the conditions under which it will be retained.

◆ Prepare a standing-order mandate for ongoing rent payments and inform utility companies of the occupier's liability to pay bills.

◆ Collect the first rent payment and deposit.

◆ Complete the check-in procedure with your tenants and obtain signatures on the inventory and tenancy agreement.

◆ Pay the stamp-duty applicable for the counterpart.

(10)

Managing the Tenancy

In this chapter:

- repairing obligations
- inspections
- harassment and illegal eviction
- managing late rent and arrears.

Scottish-born American author, Amelia E. Barr, wrote:

> *Events that are predestined require but little management. They manage themselves. They slip into place while we sleep, and suddenly we are aware that the thing we fear to attempt, is already accomplished.*

Some landlords believe they can leave their tenancies to progress to expiry without intervention. In reality, this premise results in being unprepared for the problems that can occur. Be aware of your responsibilities, plan ahead, equip yourself for difficulties that may arise, and your tenancy will be more fortuitous and less prone to calamity.

REPAIRING OBLIGATIONS

The Landlord and Tenant Act 1985 makes landlords responsible for most repairs of a dwelling let for less than seven years. This is **statute law** and cannot be undermined by contrary terms entered in a tenancy agreement. The Act means that you will usually have to undertake repairs, when required, to:

- the structure and exterior of the dwelling
- basins, sinks, baths, and other sanitary installations
- systems and appliances for providing hot water and heating.

Whilst the law is not conclusive, it is generally accepted that landlords are responsible for repairs to furniture and other appliances and equipment supplied by them. Liability should be clearly identified in the tenancy agreement for all other necessary repairs. Landlords are usually only required to **make good**, not to **improve**. A tenant recently lost his case in court because he was seeking satisfaction from a landlord who refused to install a damp-proof course to solve a problem of dampness. He lost because it was deemed the installation would be an improvement rather than a repair to something that already existed. If the landlord had refused to make good a faulty damp-proof course, the tenant would probably have won.

Tenants also have responsibilities. They must, for example, turn the water off to prevent damage if a leak occurs and guard against pipes freezing if going on holiday during winter. They should care for the dwelling and not wilfully or negligently damage it and ensure their guests and co-occupiers are equally mindful.

Prudent landlords will plan for all eventualities and have telephone numbers available of favoured electricians, plumbers and builders to remedy defects promptly.

INSPECTIONS

There is no formal requirement obliging landlords to conduct inspections during the tenancy; but there are numerous advantages to it. Landlords can:

- assess whether the property is being kept properly

- identify any repairs that are required

- identify new occupiers not recognised as tenants

- assess the tenant's intentions before expiry of the term.

Quarterly inspections on a mutually convenient date should be agreed, in advance, and confirmed in writing. A brief examination of each room and any garden area should be conducted and notes made regarding cleanliness and upkeep. Assuming you have no objection, ask the tenant whether they would like to continue occupying the property after the term has expired. Their answer will allow you to plan ahead and, where appropriate, issue notice at the required time (see Chapter 11).

Some tenants may prevent or impede you from undertaking inspections. They may have forgotten about the appointment, be irritated by the inconvenience or feel acrimonious towards you over another matter. In these circumstances, be acquiescent rather than mulish. Achieving an amicable compromise is likely to get you into the property and cause less problems, whereas a display of stubborn authoritarianism will just exacerbate any difficulties. If the tenant remains intractable, you can issue written notice (minimum of 24 hours) that you will gain access during a reasonable time of day to conduct the inspection. Always confirm that suitable provision exists in the tenancy agreement before employing this right.

HARASSMENT AND ILLEGAL EVICTION

Severe penalties can be applied to any landlord who illegally evicts or harasses their tenant (Protection from Eviction Act 1977). Be extremely careful not to cause either occurrence and be aware that unscrupulous tenants have been known to manipulate incidents purely for compensatory gain. Both statute and common law provide tenants with the right to **quiet enjoyment** of the dwelling. Any disturbance by the landlord may be construed as interfering with this right and give credence to a claim.

Examples of **harassment** might include:

♦ Using abusive or threatening language in verbal or written communications.

♦ Gaining access to the property without due notice, at unreasonable times of the day or night or for a purpose inconsistent with the terms of tenancy.

♦ Contacting the tenant's employer or bank regarding behaviour or rent arrears.

♦ Getting another person to encourage the tenant's payment of rent arrears.

♦ Any action that discourages the tenant's continued occupation or enjoyment of all or part of the dwelling, including interfering with or a withdrawal of services.

Examples of **illegal eviction** might include:

♦ Changing or adding locks on entrance doors without providing new keys.

♦ Undertaking work at the property that prevents occupation of it (unless an agreement has been reached permitting it).

♦ Terminating a tenancy without appropriate notice.

♦ Evicting a tenant without a court order.

♦ Turning off essential supplies such as water, gas or electricity, which force the tenant to vacate.

MANAGING LATE RENT AND ARREARS

Rent is due by midnight on the day specified by the tenancy agreement or, when no date is indicated, the last day of the period. You must keep a record of all underpayments, late payments and non-payments of rent, as these can provide essential evidence if you later need to pursue possession of your property. Good record-keeping will also allow you to keep track of the tenant's account and identify the balance outstanding at any particular time. As soon as a payment is overdue, bring it to the tenant's attention by writing to them (keeping a copy for your files). If the tenancy involves a guarantor, send them a copy of the letter and remind them of their responsibility to meet any overdue amount.

There is no need to send any additional letters at this stage, even if the rent goes unpaid for the full duration of the period (weekly or monthly), but ensure you send one letter for *every* unpaid amount. The significance of maintaining accurate records and keeping written evidence of arrears will become clear when we examine how you go about obtaining possession in the next chapter.

An assured shorthold tenant may decide to purposely **withhold** rent because:

♦ a requested repair or replacement is outstanding;

♦ they have paid an expense they believe the landlord is liable for; or

♦ the end of tenancy has been reached and they have withheld the last month's rent in lieu of the deposit.

In each situation the rent remains lawfully due and this should be made clear to the tenant in writing. By withholding rent, they are breaking a fundamental obligation in the agreement and jeopardising their security of tenure as a result. However, under common law, the tenant can employ a procedure known as **set off** in certain circumstances. If a landlord is in breach of their repairing obligations, the tenant can obtain estimates and present them to the landlord. The tenant *must* advise the landlord that, if the work is not conducted within a set period, they intend to arrange it and pay the bill from rent due or owed.

If the landlord has started the process of seeking possession due to rent arrears, the tenant can set off arrears against repair costs *providing* the arrears are purely the result of the landlord's failure to deal with the repairs (i.e. arrears did not occur prior to the repairs becoming necessary).

SUMMARY

+ Once a repair or replacement for which you are responsible is reported or identified, deal with it promptly.

+ Undertake regular inspections of the property, giving advance written notice of at least 24 hours.

+ Do not undertake any action which may be construed as harassment or illegal eviction.

+ Keep adequate records of late or underpaid rent and arrears. Write to the tenant as soon as payment is overdue, reminding them of their obligations.

(11)

End of Tenancy

In this chapter:

- planning for tenancy expiry
- issuing notice
- check-out
- dilapidations and deposit refund
- statutory periodic tenancy
- grounds for possession
- accelerated possession procedure.

An assured shorthold tenancy ends by notice, forfeiture or surrender (the latter being where *both* parties agree to early termination); or because it naturally expires at the end of the term. However, even though a tenancy has ended, the landlord cannot force their tenant to leave the premises. This is a golden rule of letting and landlords who disregard it do so at their peril.

PLANNING FOR TENANCY EXPIRY

At least *two months* prior to the end of the tenancy term, a landlord must assess what they and their tenant want to happen at expiry. If the tenant wishes to continue his occupation (and the landlord has no objection), the landlord can:

- create a new assured shorthold to commence following expiry of the current one (and with a new rent if desired); or

◆ allow the term to expire, in which case the tenancy would automatically continue as a **statutory periodic tenancy** with the same terms and conditions as the original. This type of tenancy runs according to the periodic nature of rent payments (usually month to month).

Alternatively, if the landlord wishes to bring the tenancy to an end at expiry of the current term, they must serve *at least two months'* notice (see below).

ISSUING NOTICE

If the landlord does *not* want a statutory periodic tenancy to be automatically created at the end of the term, they must serve due notice (according to the Housing Act 1988) to their assured shorthold tenant. The tenant, on the other hand, does not normally have to serve notice to end their obligations and leave at the end of the term, unless the tenancy agreement makes it a requirement.

The form of notice is called **Section 21 – Notice Requiring Possession.** These can be obtained from a legal stationer (a free version is available from **www.letonthenet.com**). Section 21 of the Housing Act 1988 describes the rules for notice issued **during the fixed term** and those for **after the fixed term has expired** (i.e. during a statutory periodic tenancy). We will deal here with the former only, Section 21(1)(b). To serve notice, you should complete the following procedure *exactly*:

1. Obtain a notice form.

2. Complete it with the details for tenant name (all joint tenants must be named on the notice), your own name and address, and the tenanted property address.

3. **Date possession is required by**: enter the last day of the tenancy term (this can in fact be for any time *at or after* expiry of the term *providing* the two-month rule below is followed *and* service is made within the tenancy term, including the last day of tenancy).

4a. **Date of notice**: enter the current date, *providing* it is *at least* two months before the date at 3 above (notice can be served at any time once the tenancy has begun, but it must always be at least two months prior to the possession date – but see 4b below); *and* providing you intend delivering it to the tenant(s) on the same day. If you intend posting the notice, add three days to the notice period to allow for delivery.

4b. If the tenancy rent periods are quarterly the minimum notice is three months; if six months or more, then six months' notice.

5. Sign the notice.

6. Make two copies of the completed notice for your files.

7. Serve the notice by hand or by post (ordinary first class post unless the tenancy agreement dictates something else). It is essential that you arrange for a witness when delivery is made in person. The courts accept that notice has been served if it has been delivered to the let property address (it does not have to be handed to the tenant in person).

For serving notice *during* the fixed term and for reasons other than the natural expiry of the assured shorthold term, see grounds for possession later in this chapter.

CHECK-OUT

On the last day of tenancy, after the tenant has removed their possessions and vacated, you should:

♦ Receive the keys and details of their forwarding address.

♦ Read gas, electricity and water meters, and inform all utility companies and the council-tax department that they have vacated (provide them with the tenant's new address for any final bills).

♦ Check that any telephone line has been disconnected.

♦ Turn water stop-taps, heating and hot water systems off and drain water tanks (if appropriate and according to the weather conditions).

♦ Inspect the property thoroughly for losses, damage and cleanliness, using the inventory for guidance (make notes and take photographs of any adverse observations).

♦ For security purposes, consider changing the locks and/or intruder alarm code.

♦ Install your 'to let' boards and begin marketing for new tenants.

If the tenant fails to vacate on the last day of tenancy you will need to seek possession through the courts (see Grounds for Possession and Accelerated Possession Procedure).

DILAPIDATIONS AND DEPOSIT REFUND

Providing the tenant has paid the rent in full, paid all utility bills and has returned the property in good condition (fair wear and tear excepted), return the tenant's deposit promptly.

However, the landlord is entitled to deduct the appropriate sum for any reinstatement, cleaning or repairs deemed necessary, and the reimbursement of any outstanding rent arrears, in accordance with the terms of the tenancy agreement. When calculating the cost of these, the landlord should:

◆ Be fair and objective in their assessment and seek a second opinion where possible.

◆ Obtain several estimates for any repairs, purchases or services required.

◆ Obtain copies of outstanding utility bills (but see below).

◆ Deduct a depreciation amount according to age and condition when replacing items damaged or lost.

◆ Write to the tenant explaining the reasons for deductions and seek their approval before proceeding (not absolutely necessary, but useful in maintaining an amicable relationship).

◆ Act quickly and efficiently in dealing with the deposit, but not to the detriment of your assessment of costs for reinstatement of the property.

If damage and other tenant liable expenses exceed the deposit, consider using the Small Claims Court to recover the balance (if the amount is disputed or unpaid after notification and is £5,000 or less). Check the tenant's obligations in the tenancy agreement before going to court. This is particularly relevant with unpaid utility bills, because recovery of payments may not be possible if the liability contract existed only between the tenant and the service providers involved.

STATUTORY PERIODIC TENANCY

A statutory periodic tenancy (SPT) arises if the landlord fails to intervene at the end of an assured shorthold tenancy (AST) *and* where the tenant stays in occupation. It is *automatic*; no additional documentation is required. The original terms and obligations of the AST continue as before. This arrangement can have advantages for the landlord and tenant because, as there is no fixed term, there is greater flexibility when either party wants the tenancy to end.

The landlord can terminate a SPT tenancy at any time by giving two months' written notice (but see below). The tenant has the same right, though their notice only needs to be one full rent period. To serve notice [Section 21(4)(a)], the landlord should follow the same procedure as before but with the following exception:

♦ A minimum of two months' notice (three months for quarterly rent payments; six months for six monthly rent payments) must be given *after* the AST has expired *and* with the expiry of notice being on the last day of a tenancy period. The tenancy period depends on the payment of rent. To calculate the date correctly (this is very important), you must refer to the original AST agreement. The SPT begins the day after the AST expires. So if it expires on 20 October, the SPT begins on 21 October. If the rent is monthly, then the last day of the first tenancy period in this example is 20 November, with subsequent periods also ending on 20. Using this example, if you served notice on 5 November the tenancy would not end until 20 January.

It is easy to make mistakes when calculating notice dates, which is why I advised earlier in this book against using certain tenancy start dates or varying the rent collection day. Precision is important because errors can lead to unsuccessful possession proceedings if taken to court.

GROUNDS FOR POSSESSION

Although issuing notice, done correctly, will bring the AST or SPT to an end, it does not automatically give the landlord possession. Eviction requires a court order. If the tenancy term has ended, the landlord does not need to apply to court under any of the **grounds** set out below and can instead use the **accelerated possession procedure** (see later in this chapter).

However, to apply for a court order *during the tenancy term*, they must issue a (Section 8) Notice Seeking Possession and satisfy the court that they have a right to possession under one or more of the grounds. With AST tenants, landlords can only apply using Grounds 2, 8, 10 to 15 or 17, during the fixed term. This involves following a strict procedure and, in the case of discretionary grounds, success is not guaranteed. There are 17 grounds for possession falling into two distinct categories. They can be applied singularly or in combination:

◆ **Mandatory grounds** (1 to 8): the court *must* grant possession if the ground is proved by the landlord.

◆ **Discretionary grounds** (9 to 17): the court *may* grant possession if the ground is proved by the landlord.

The grounds for possession are:

(*Note*: Grounds 1 to 5 are *prior notice grounds* where the landlord must have issued notice to the tenant *before the tenancy began or at commencement*, that they may seek possession using that ground.)

Ground 1: The landlord lived in or intends to live in the property as their only or principal home.

Ground 2: The property is mortgaged and the lender wants possession (the loan must have started prior to the tenancy).

Ground 3: The tenancy fixed period is eight months or less and within 12 months of the tenancy starting it was let for a holiday.

Ground 4: The tenancy is a student-letting and within 12 months of the tenancy starting it was let to students by an educational establishment.

Ground 5: The property is held for use by a minister of religion and is now required for that purpose.

Ground 6: Substantial redevelopment of the property is intended which cannot be undertaken while the tenant is occupying it. This ground cannot be used if the property was purchased with an existing tenant.

Ground 7: The former tenant has died and no one has a right of succession to the tenancy.

Ground 8: The tenant owes at least two months' rent (if rent is paid monthly) or eight weeks' rent (if weekly), both when notice seeking possession is issued *and* at the time of the court hearing.

Ground 9: There is suitable alternative accommodation available (tenant's removal costs must be paid).

Ground 10: The tenant was behind with the rent when notice was served seeking possession *and* when court proceedings started.

Ground 11: The tenant has been persistently late in paying rent even though they were not behind with payments when possession proceedings began.

Ground 12: The tenant has broken one or more of the tenancy conditions (does not apply to rent payments).

Ground 13: The property has deteriorated due to the behaviour of the tenant or any other person living in it.

Ground 14: The tenant or someone visiting or living in the property has caused, or is likely to cause, a nuisance or annoyance to neighbours or anyone visiting the locality. Or they have been convicted of using the property or allowing it to be used for immoral or illegal purposes, or for an arrestable offence, committed in the property or locality.

Ground 15: The furniture has deteriorated because it has been ill-treated by the tenant or any other person living in the property.

Ground 16: The tenancy was given because the tenant was previously employed by you or a former landlord, but is no longer being employed.

Ground 17: The tenancy was granted based on a false statement knowingly or recklessly made by the tenant, or by someone acting at the tenant's instigation.

Notice must be given to the tenant *before* starting court proceedings. The 'Section 8' notice period varies according to the ground(s) being used:

- For Grounds 3, 4, 8, 10, 11, 12, 13, 15 or 17 at least two weeks' notice must be given.

- For Grounds 1, 2, 5, 6, 7, 9 and 16 at least two months' notice must be given. If the tenancy is a SPT, then the notice period must end on the last day of a period. In addition, the notice period must be at least as long as the tenancy period, for example three months in the case of rent being paid quarterly (but limited to six months for a yearly tenancy period).

- For Ground 14 there is no notice period. Court proceedings can start as soon as notice is issued.

Section 8 Notice forms can be obtained from legal stationers and on-line at **www.letlink.co.uk**, **www.landlordlaw.co.uk** or **www.legalhelpers.co.uk** The same rules apply for completing the form as for the Section 21 notice, except that you must enter the ground(s) under which possession is being sought and explain the circumstances why the ground is being cited. You must enter the wording of the ground *exactly* as it appears in the Housing Act (obtain copies of the 1988 and 1996 Acts from your local HMSO for reference). *Note*: the text descriptions above are *not* as written in the Acts; they have been condensed for easier understanding.

When notice is being issued because of rent arrears, a schedule of the arrears should accompany the notice *and* it must be in a format acceptable to the courts. The standard County Court process is often slow and bureaucratic and many landlords are reluctant to use it. As one small mistake can cost you the entire case, it is wise to consider employing a solicitor experienced in property matters to assist and guide you. If the tenant fails to remedy the breach or it is one that cannot be remedied, the landlord has 12 months in which to commence court proceedings for possession.

ACCELERATED POSSESSION PROCEDURE

The accelerated possession procedure (APP) was introduced to help streamline the process for landlords seeking possession of their property. Although it does not always live up to expectations, it is easier than the standard process. However, the APP cannot be used to recover rent arrears. For assured shorthold tenancies, the APP can only be used at the end of the fixed term or during a periodic tenancy *and* a Section 21 Notice must first have been issued. All the necessary forms and a set of guidance notes can be obtained from the County Court or on-line at **www.courtservice.gov.uk**

Remember that, even after successfully obtaining a possession order from the court, the tenant *still* cannot be evicted by his landlord. The landlord must first seek a warrant from the court. The court will then arrange for bailiffs to perform the eviction. Taking defaulting tenants to court is usually best avoided, if at all possible, but the APP provides a fast-track legal solution for those situations that demand it.

SUMMARY

+ Issue notice at the appropriate time to bring the assured shorthold tenancy to an end, unless you want a statutory periodic tenancy to arise automatically.

+ Choose the Section 21 Notice route, when seeking possession, in preference to the more protracted Section 8 Notice method.

+ Assess dilapidations fairly and objectively at the end of tenancy and return the tenant's deposit (or balance of) as quickly as possible.

+ Avoid going to court unless absolutely necessary but, if there is no alternative and circumstances are appropriate, consider using the Accelerated Possession Procedure to regain possession.

+ Get help and advice from landlords who have experience of using the court service or consider employing a solicitor to assist you when undertaking legal action to recover your property.

(12)

Letting in Scotland

In this chapter:

- ◆ legislation affecting Scottish landlords
- ◆ short assured tenancy
- ◆ the deposit
- ◆ safety inspections
- ◆ extending the tenancy
- ◆ ending a short assured tenancy
- ◆ seeking possession
- ◆ houses in multiple occupation
- ◆ further information.

Landlords letting property in Scotland are governed by laws and regulations that vary from those for England and Wales. Whilst the main principles and framework are similar, there are fundamental differences of which landlords should be aware. These include:

LEGISLATION AFFECTING SCOTTISH LANDLORDS

Most new tenancies created after 2 January 1989 are governed by Part II of the Housing (Scotland) Act 1988. It introduced **assured** tenancies which are similar in design to those for England and Wales. There are, however, critical differences in the way these tenancies are named, established, managed and terminated. The Housing (Scotland) Act 2001 introduced some changes in definition, particularly relating to disability and discrimination, but the Scottish Executive have confirmed these have not altered significantly the aspects of tenancy introduced by the 1988 Act.

SHORT ASSURED TENANCY

A **short assured tenancy** (SAT) is comparable to the '**assured shorthold tenancy**' in England and Wales. There are two major disparities:

- The landlord must give to the tenant, *before* any agreement is signed, a notice (called AT5) that the tenancy being proposed is to be a SAT. If notice is not properly issued, the resulting tenancy will be the **assured** type, affording the tenant far greater security of tenure than was probably intended. The notice can be obtained from a law stationer or on-line at **www.scotland.gov.uk/housing**

- The tenancy must be for a minimum fixed term of six months.

The tenancy agreement *must* be in writing and a copy has to be given to the tenant. There is no scope for a verbal agreement and landlords are unable to charge a fee for providing the document. If a tenant is not given a written agreement or receives one that does not reflect the terms of tenancy, they can ask the Sheriff to have one drawn up or apply for a revision of existing terms.

THE DEPOSIT

In Scotland, landlords cannot demand more than a sum equal to two months' rent as a surety deposit. In addition, it is generally forbidden to ask for a premium or key-money in granting, renewing, continuing or assigning an assured or short assured tenancy and a fine of up to £400 is applicable to those that do.

SAFETY INSPECTIONS

The regulations for electrical and gas safety, and for furnishings, are the same as those outlined previously for England and Wales.

EXTENDING THE TENANCY

SATs can continue beyond the expiry date of the fixed term. If the landlord and tenant do not intervene (that is, they do nothing at all at expiry of the initial term), a new period of tenancy will be created automatically which will be equal in length to the first period. This subsequent period is called a **continued short assured tenancy** (CSAT).

Alternatively, the landlord can create a new SAT if the tenant agrees. The new SAT is not subject to the same set-up procedure as the original. There is no requirement to serve a new AT5 notice and there is no minimum term.

ENDING A SHORT ASSURED TENANCY

The landlord must issue a **notice to quit**. The period of notice depends on the nature of rent payments, that is, the periodic structure of the tenancy. If the property is let:

- weekly, fortnightly or monthly, then at least four weeks' notice must be given; or

- quarterly, then at least 31 days' notice must be given; or

- yearly, then at least 40 days' notice must be given.

Notice cannot take effect earlier than the expiry date of the agreement and must contain prescribed information for the tenant in accordance with the Housing Act, otherwise it will be invalid. Issuing a notice to quit is appropriate prior to granting the tenant a new SAT or as a first step to seeking possession. It brings the current tenancy to an end (at expiry of the term), but it does not mean the tenant has to leave the property. As with letting in England and Wales, a tenant cannot be evicted without a court order.

SEEKING POSSESSION

To seek possession, landlords must issue formal notice *(Form AT6:Notice of Proceedings)*. For SATs, notice does not need to be submitted on an AT6 form, though it can be used, but must contain the **grounds** specified in the Housing (Scotland) Act 1988 through which possession is being sought. The **Notice to quit** and the **Notice of proceedings** can be issued together, subject to the minimum notice periods. The minimum notice period when seeking possession under grounds 1, 2, 5, 6, 7, 9 or 17 is two months. For any other ground, it is two weeks (but be aware that the Notice to quit has a minimum of 28 days).

The Grounds for Possession are almost identical to those described in Chapter 11 except:

♦ **Ground 8:** the tenant must be in *three months* arrears of rent when the notice of proceedings is served and at the date of the hearing.

♦ **Ground 10:** the *tenant* has given the landlord a Notice to Quit, which has expired, but has continued to occupy the property. The landlord can use this ground providing they seek an order for possession within six months of the notice expiring.

◆ **Ground 12:** some rent remains outstanding at the beginning of court proceedings *and* at the time Notice of Proceedings is served.

◆ **Ground 13:** the tenant has broken one or more obligations of tenancy other than any involving the payment of rent.

◆ **Ground 14:** as Ground 13 of the Housing Act 1988 for England and Wales.

◆ **Ground 15:** as Ground 14 of the Housing Act 1988 for England and Wales.

◆ **Ground 16:** as Ground 15 of the Housing Act 1988 for England and Wales.

◆ **Ground 17:** as Ground 16 of the Housing Act 1988 for England and Wales.

There is no equivalent ground in Scottish law to seek possession because a tenancy was granted based on false statements. In addition, there is no equivalent fast-track method of regaining possession in Scotland, unlike the Accelerated Possession Procedure available in England and Wales. Landlords are advised to obtain the exact wording of the grounds in the Housing (Scotland) Act 1988 when quoting them for possession purposes. Always remember that a tenant cannot be evicted unless an Order for Possession has been granted by the Sheriff.

HOUSES IN MULTIPLE OCCUPATION (HMOS)
HMO landlords tend to be dealt with punitively under Scot-

tish law. It is a harsh, complex and bureaucratic regime. By tightening the definition of what constitutes a HMO and by inflicting strict regulations through local authority imposed minimum standards, the Scottish Parliament stated its intention to *'get rid of slum landlords!'*. Although this will undoubtedly be one of the results, it has also increased the supply and maintenance costs for HMO landlords.

On 1 October 2000, a compulsory licensing scheme was introduced for all HMO landlords ['Civic Government (Scotland) Act (Licensing of Houses in Multiple Occupation) Order 2000']. Local authorities were granted powers to impose standards, which differ from one authority to another, about the condition of the building and how it is managed. The scheme was introduced gradually over three years. After 1 October 2003, where more than two unrelated people share a property, it will be considered a HMO. The exemptions include registered homes, residential care homes, private hospitals and residential accommodation for school students.

Landlords concerned about HMOs and licensing should consult the local authority (where their property is situated) for further information and advice *before* creating a tenancy.

FURTHER INFORMATION
The Housing (Scotland) Act 1988 can be obtained from a local HMSO or on-line at **www.hmso.gov.uk**

Tenancy documents and notices can be obtained from a law stationer. There are also versions available on the internet, for example **www.easylet.freeserve.co.uk** offers sample agreements from £2 each.

There are multiple internet links for legal information about renting in Scotland at **www.scottishlaw.org.uk**

The Scottish Executive provides information and free leaflets useful to landlords. These can be viewed on-line at **www.scotland.gov.uk/housing/leaflets** or by contacting them at:

Scottish Executive Development Department
Victoria Quay
Edinburgh EH6 6QQ
Tel: 08457 741 741

Other valuable information is available from:

Citizens Advice Scotland
26 George Square
Edinburgh EH8 9LD
Tel: 0131 667 0156
Website: **www.cas.org.uk**

Scottish Letting Agency
Tel: 01224 872963
Website: **www.scottish-letting-agency.com**

Scottish Association of Landlords
Gladstone House
6a Mill Lane
Edinburgh EH6 6TJ
Tel: 0131 555 5911
Website: **wwwscottishlandlords.com**

SUMMARY

◆ Be aware of the different legislation affecting landlords in Scotland.

◆ To create a short assured tenancy you must issue an AT5 Notice to the tenant before signing the agreement.

◆ To prevent a continued short assured tenancy being automatically created, with the same length of term as the original, you must issue a Notice to Quit at the appropriate time prior to expiry of the short assured term.

◆ Houses in multiple occupation are subject to a strict licensing scheme. Landlords should be aware of the HMO definition, enforced minimum standards, and other regulations affecting them, before starting a tenancy.

(13)

Troubleshooting

In this chapter:

- ◆ absentee tenants
- ◆ neighbour disputes
- ◆ succession by husband or wife
- ◆ landlords living outside the UK
- ◆ receiving/sending documents by fax and e-mail
- ◆ under-18s.

This section explains some of the most common predicaments faced by landlords.

ABSENTEE TENANTS

There is nothing more frustrating than a tenant in arrears of rent and *apparently* absent from the property. The landlord is faced with a dilemma: *has the tenant vacated permanently or do they intend to return?* It may be that they are:

- ◆ on holiday
- ◆ in hospital
- ◆ visiting friends
- ◆ working away from home or
- ◆ in prison.

Taking possession of the property, changing locks or re-letting it to alternative tenants may result in alarming and expensive consequences should the absent tenant return. Any action preventing the tenant's access to or occupation of the dwelling, without a court order, is likely to be a breach of the Protection from Eviction Act 1977. *There is no maximum fine* for such an offence. There are actions landlords can take, but these should be done quickly and thoroughly to corroborate suspicions:

1. Issue written 24 hours notice of your intention to inspect the property and keep a copy for your files. Hand-deliver this through the letter-box of the property with a witness.

2. At inspection, look for irrefutable evidence that the tenant has moved out. Are any of their possessions still in the property? Is there food in the kitchen? Is mail stacked behind the door?

3. Try to contact the tenant at their place of work or through relatives and friends whose details were given at application. If you succeed in making contact and the tenant confirms they no longer wish to live in the dwelling, ask for their voluntary **surrender of tenancy** in writing.

4. Talk to neighbours and ask when they last saw or spoke to the tenant.

5. Gather as much information as possible and maintain a diary of the times you called at the property or attempted to contact the tenant by telephone.

If, despite your efforts, there remains even the slightest doubt that the tenant may return to reclaim occupation:

6. Issue formal notice to bring the tenancy to an end, if applicable, and/or seek possession through the courts using the accelerated possession procedure (subject to 'ground' limitations).

NEIGHBOUR DISPUTES

If neighbours complain about the behaviour of your tenant:

◆ Obtain the complaint in writing.

◆ Get both sides of the argument and assess the validity of complaint.

◆ Write to the tenant and explain their obligations under the tenancy agreement.

◆ Provide a 'cooling off' period to see whether matters improve.

◆ Ask the local authority if they offer a mediation service for neighbours in dispute and, where excessive noise is being caused, consult the environmental health department.

◆ If all else fails, consider issuing notice to bring a statutory periodic tenancy to an end or seek possession through the courts via grounds 12 and 14 (discretionary) for assured shorthold tenancies during the fixed term.

SUCCESSION BY HUSBAND OR WIFE

When couples have a joint tenancy and one decides to vacate, the status of each party is unchanged under the terms of the agreement. Both remain equally liable to pay the rent. Sometimes an amicable arrangement will be made between the parties and the landlord which brings the former tenancy to an end (by mutually agreeing 'surrender'), allowing the remaining partner to continue occupation under a new tenancy.

However, congenial determinations are not always so easy to achieve. They are particularly problematic in matters regarding separation and divorce or the death of one partner *and* where the tenancy is not jointly held. The landlord must consider carefully what **succession** rights apply to the remaining or surviving partner (if not the original tenant). Above all else, they must ensure they do not inadvertently harass or illegally evict the individual by misunderstanding their status and legal entitlement.

If it is a statutory periodic tenancy and the tenant dies, the surviving spouse, or anyone who was living with the tenant as husband or wife, has an automatic right to succeed to the tenancy. There can, however, only be one succession in this instance. If the surviving spouse dies, the tenancy ends. However, during an assured shorthold tenancy, the executors of the deceased's estate will decide whether anyone has a claim to the tenancy.

Matters involving separation and divorce are dealt with in a slightly different manner. In some circumstances, the Family Law Act 1996 provides limited security of tenure for the partner or cohabitee when the tenant-partner has vacated the property. An **occupation order** or **order of transfer** is usually made during matrimonial court proceedings and landlords are advised to deal direct with the remaining partner's appointed solicitor, to obtain appropriate information.

LANDLORDS LIVING OUTSIDE THE UNITED KINGDOM

Many people choose to leave the UK to live, work or retire abroad. This applies to landlords too, but they must make special provisions for their tenants and inform the Inland Revenue before doing so. The usual arrangement is for an agent to be appointed who will collect and distribute rent and deal with day-to-day management issues. Landlords living abroad should be aware that:

◆ Tenants have a legal right to the name and address of their landlord, regardless of where they are residing.

◆ When employing the Accelerated Possession Procedure, agents cannot sign the form N5B on behalf of the non-resident landlord (a solicitor will need to be appointed to represent them instead).

◆ Unless a landlord has applied for and received an 'exemption certificate' from the Inland Revenue's Financial Intermediaries and Claims Office (FICO), the agent (or tenant if rent is paid direct to the landlord) will be responsible for deducting the landlord's tax from the rent. There are, in addition, routine forms to complete and annual reports have to be submitted. For more information, contact FICO on 0151 472 6000.

RECEIVING/SENDING DOCUMENTS BY FAX AND E-MAIL

Most written material sent by fax or e-mail can be held as legal evidence in a court of law. There are countless examples on public record. Precedent was probably set in the 1980s by the Oliver North, Iran/contra affair, where electronic mail was accepted as admissible evidence in court. As the use of this medium became more widespread, the UK legal system had to consider and acknowledge the validity of cyber-text and make judgement on what constitutes a signature. Various Acts of Parliament have since cited the electronic medium and confirmed it as an applicable form of *legal* communication.

When sending or receiving anything by fax or e-mail consider the following:

◆ Tenancy documents and notices that are required to be in **prescribed form** must correspond with the criteria laid down in the Housing Act 1988 (as amended by the Housing Act 1996). This means that they must have a particular layout or include predetermined phrases to be legitimate.

◆ The Electronic Communications Act 2000 makes digital signatures legally binding in most circumstances. The signature does not necessarily have to be handwritten. It can be typed, but it should be certified by the author as originating from him or her and be issued with legal intent.

◆ The Defamation Act 1996 makes it an offence to disseminate defamatory statements. Phrases acceptable to you may be interpreted as being offensive by someone else. In addition, as e-mails can be submitted to court as evidence, statements issued may also be misconstrued as harassment (see Chapter 10).

UNDER-18s

The law does not prevent a landlord letting their property to someone under the age of 18. However, a **minor** cannot be bound by contract and difficulties may therefore arise if there is a breach of the tenancy terms. For example, a tenant aged 17 may be obliged to pay rent but, if they fail to do so, the landlord cannot seek satisfaction through the courts as they could with someone aged 18 or over.

Although this dilemma is probably best avoided, it *can* be resolved by securing a guarantor (see Chapter 7). The application of a watertight Guarantor Agreement is essential in this situation and a solicitor will be able to assist in devising one pertinent to your needs. Guarantors should be fully referenced and made liable for all of the tenant's obligations should default occur.

Glossary

Note: This glossary must be considered within the context of property letting and, particularly, in relation to assured shorthold tenancies unless otherwise defined.

Accelerated possession. A fast-track legal procedure for seeking possession through the courts in England and Wales.

Affidavit. A statement of fact made in writing and verified by oath, before someone with the authority to administer it (usually a solicitor).

Assign. The transfer of legal title or interest, for example a tenant passing their entitlement to occupy a property to another person. Assignment is usually prohibited by the tenancy agreement.

Assured shorthold tenancy. A tenancy defined by the Housing Act 1988 (as amended by the Housing Act 1996) granted by a landlord to a tenant for a fixed period. This is the most common form of residential tenancy in England and Wales. Landlords can obtain possession of their property (after six months through the courts), if they wish, subject to the fixed-term expiring and proper notice being issued.

Assured tenancy. A tenancy defined by the Housing Act 1988 (as amended by the Housing 1996) granted by a private landlord to a private tenant in England and Wales. Assured tenants have the right to remain in the property unless the landlord can prove to the court that there are grounds for possession. There is no automatic right to possession when the tenancy ends.

Bailiff. An officer of the court with the authority to enforce possession orders.

Bank draft. A secure form of payment that looks like a cheque but is guaranteed by the payee's bank.

Break clause. A clause in a tenancy agreement that allows the tenant and/or the landlord the right to bring the tenancy to an end before its normal expiry date. Break clauses usually specify the conditions and notice period required.

British Standard. The display of a British Standard number (e.g. BS 1234) on, for example, a consumer product, shows that the manufacturer claims to have made it in accordance with the British Standard. If accompanied by the letters EN and/or ISO, it was developed as a (EN) European or (ISO) international standard, then adopted by the UK as a British Standard.

Buy-to-let. A scheme originally promoted by ARLA (Association of Residential Letting Agents) which eventually introduced mortgages designed specifically for landlords. Most banks and building societies now offer variations of this type of loan. The maximum loan-to-value (LTV) is often lower but, unlike an ordinary mortgage, rental income is taken into consideration by the lender when calculating the amount offered.

Capital gains tax. A liability incurred, according to the level of profit gained, when an increase in property value has been realised. An individual's permanent home is usually exempt, but additional homes and letting-units are not.

Capital growth. The rise in value of a property over time.

Carbon monoxide. An odourless invisible poisonous gas (CO_1) produced through the incomplete combustion of carbon-based fuels. Yellow-coloured or smoky gas-fire and gas-boiler flames suggest the presence of CO_1 and their operation should be discontinued immediately to prevent potentially fatal consequences.

Company let. A letting to a company (rather than an individual) cannot be 'assured' under the Housing Act 1988 and, as a result, such tenants generally have less security of tenure. Company-let agreements are widely available and create a usually straightforward contractual arrangement between landlord and tenant.

Contract. A legally binding agreement between two or more parties.

Corgi. The Council for Registered Gas Installers. Engineers who conduct gas-safety inspections for landlords must be registered.

Counterpart agreement. A duplicate of the tenancy agreement, retained by the landlord and having the tenant's signature on it (the tenant retains the agreement containing the landlord's signature).

Covenant. A promise made in a legal document which can be positive or restrictive (for example, making it an obligation to perform or, conversely, prohibit certain actions).

Demised premises. The part or parts of the property where the tenant or lessee has legal right to exclusive possession.

Deposit. A sum held as security against certain events and for a set period. The 'events' might include rent arrears, damage, loss, and the reinstatement of decoration and cleanliness (fair wear and tear excluded). The tenancy agreement normally specifies which events are covered by the deposit and whether interest will be paid.

Dilapidations. This refers to a state of disrepair for which the tenant is legally accountable. The tenancy agreement should describe the extent of the tenant's liability and the landlord must have suffered or will suffer financial loss due to the disrepair. The cost of dilapidations is usually deducted from the tenant's deposit at the end of the tenancy.

Display label. All new furniture must carry a display label at the point of sale, except mattresses and bed-bases, pillows, cushions and seat pads, loose covers and stretch covers. These labels provide information about the product's compliance with the 1988 safety regulations.

Eviction. The process by which a tenant is prevented or removed from physical possession of the property. Legal eviction can only be performed with a court order and by officers approved by the court.

Exclusive possession. A legal right to occupy the property and exclude others from it.

Express obligations. These are the promises made by tenant and landlord within the terms of the tenancy agreement. They are secondary to **implied obligations** imposed by common law and statute.

Fair wear and tear. The normal day-to-day deterioration of decoration, furnishings and fittings, that occur over time and are distinct from dilapidations. Tenants are not usually made liable for fair wear and tear.

Fittings. These are usually mobile items or things that can be removed easily from the property, not forming part of the structure or fabric of the dwelling.

Fixtures. These are 'fixed' elements, the removal of which would be likely to cause damage to the fabric of walls, ceilings, floors, windows or doors.

Forfeiture. The tenant 'forfeits' their tenancy when a landlord brings it to an end because of a breach of the terms, for example, due to the non-payment of rent. Although under certain circumstances and following a set procedure, the landlord has the right to bring the tenancy to an end, the tenant cannot be evicted without an order from the court.

Freehold. A property and/or land held indefinitely (owned forever) with no other person or agency having greater interest.

Furnished. There is no legal definition of what constitutes a furnished dwelling. However, tenants looking for 'furnished' property generally expect all of the following items to be supplied: seating, beds, wardrobes, tables, white goods, light fittings, carpets and curtains.

Gas flue. An installation through which the waste gases of combustion pass to the exterior of the property. Most modern gas appliances require a flue.

Gas safety certificate. A document issued by a CORGI registered installer confirming the inspection and safety of gas installations, flues and appliances, and their associated pipework. Copies of the certificate must be given to each new tenant *before* occupation *and* within 28 days of an inspection being undertaken. Testing must be conducted annually.

Gearing. The process whereby investors use property as security to acquire funding, so that further properties can be purchased. Gearing brings a better return when the total yield plus capital growth exceeds the borrowing rate.

Gross rental income. The total income from letting the property before deductions for tax and expenditure.

Grounds for possession. The 17 'grounds' contained in the Housing Act 1988 (as amended by the Housing Act 1996) through which landlords can apply to court for possession of their property. Mandatory grounds are those where the court must grant a possession order providing the ground is proved. Discretionary grounds are those where the court can take other matters into consideration before considering whether to grant a possession order.

Guarantor. Someone who agrees to accept the liability for some or all of the tenant's obligations if the tenant defaults on rent payments or other terms of tenancy.

Headlessor. The individual, company, group, institution or agency, who establish, govern and apply the terms of a lease upon the lessees of leasehold properties.

Holding over. A situation where a tenant remains in occupation despite the tenancy having ended or expiry of the term having passed and with no new tenancy or term being granted.

Housing benefit. An allowance available to those on low income and who satisfy the criteria. Housing benefit (H/b) is intended to pay for all or some of the rent. It is funded by government and administered by local authorities. Applicants can request a **pre-tenancy determination** to be undertaken by the rent officer service prior to considering a tenancy from a private landlord.

Housing Acts. These are the Acts of Parliament containing the definitions and rules for private residential letting in England and Wales. The 1980 Act first introduced the **shorthold** concept. The 1985 Act consolidated various statutory provisions and provided a definition for 'houses in multiple occupation'. The 1988 Act introduced assured and assured shorthold tenancies. The 1996 Act refined the existing provisions, removed the notice requirement for creating shorthold tenancies, and improved the landlord's possession rights.

Implied obligations. The rights of tenants and landlords provided by common law and statute, contained in all leases, even if they are not written into the agreement. For example, all tenants have a right to **quiet enjoyment** of the demised premises they occupy. If an implied obligation is not specified in the terms of tenancy, then the 'usual covenant' will apply, with reference to the tenant's or landlord's right under common law or statute.

Improvements. The Landlord and Tenant Act 1985 makes landlords responsible for certain **repairs**, providing the tenancy has a fixed term of seven years or less. A repair is the reinstatement, restoration or fixing of something that is faulty. An improvement goes beyond a repair and is not usually an allowable letting expense when calculating tax.

Income tax. The liability of landlords to pay the Inland Revenue a portion of rental income profit, based on total income, over and above any personal allowance and less any permitted expenses.

Inland Revenue. The government agency responsible for the collection of tax and, where required, the inspection of accounts.

Insurance. A policy that offers protection for various eventualities in return for a payment. Landlords and tenants can obtain policies to protect rent and provide legal services, in addition to the more traditional buildings and contents provision. Most domestic policies offer inadequate terms for letting and landlords should read them carefully to ensure sufficient cover is afforded.

Intranet. A restricted version of the internet with access and information limited to a company or organisation and its employees.

Inventory clerk. A specialist who can be employed to create an inventory at the start of tenancy and offer an independent assessment of dilapidations at the end of the term.

Inventory. A record and schedule of the existence and condition of furnishings, fittings, fixtures, appliances, equipment and decoration, provided by a landlord at the start of tenancy, and used to assess dilapidations when the tenancy ends.

Joint tenancy. This is where two or more people are named as tenants on the same tenancy agreement. Joint tenants are usually **severally liable** for the rent and equally culpable for any breach of tenancy terms.

Landlord and Tenant Act. The 1985 Act consolidated the prior Landlord and Tenant Act, Housing Act and Rent Act provisions. This piece of legislation includes details of the landlord's repairing obligation and the right of tenants to information about their landlord's identity and address.

Landlord. The person, persons, company, organisation or institution who provide all or part of a property to be used and/or occupied by a tenant, usually in return for rent.

Lease. Strictly, a lease is the same as a tenancy. However, it is commonly used to describe the document an owner (more correctly, the lessee) of a leasehold property receives at the point of purchase. It specifies their rights and covenants and the period of time they can occupy and/or use the building.

Leasehold. Property that is subject to a lease.

Lessee. The person who is granted a lease by the lessor.

Lessor. The person who grants the lease to a lessee.

Licence. A licence to occupy is often given when a tenancy cannot be created, for example, where the tenant does not have exclusive use of any part of the accommodation. Licensees generally have less security of tenure than assured or assured shorthold tenants.

Management charge. A mandatory fee imposed in return for management services. Leasehold properties with common parts often have a management charge associated with them for services, such as the upkeep of external parts, cleaning and decoration of communal hallways, building insurance and garden maintenance, accounting and agency provisions.

Minor. A person under the age of 18 who cannot legally be bound by contract.

Mortgage broker. An intermediary who identifies and advises on the best value mortgages available and deals with the administration involved, in return for a fee. Brokers do not sell their own products and those offered may be restricted in volume and variety.

Mortgage. In theory, a loan granted to assist with the purchase of property; in practice, a mortgagee does not own the property outright until the loan is repaid and instead becomes the lessee, hence the mortgage company has the right to repossess the property if payments are not maintained.

Multiple occupation. A house in multiple occupation is defined in Section 345 of the Housing Act 1985 as a *'house occupied by persons who do not form a single household'*. Local authorities interpret the definition differently but, once a property is identified as being in multiple occupation, it must conform to certain standards of fitness and safety.

Net rental income. The income gained from a let property after deducting expenses.

Non-resident. For tax purposes, a non-resident landlord (NRL) is one who lets property in the United Kingdom but lives overseas for six months or more. Unless the NRL has received an exemption certificate from the Inland Revenue, their letting-agent (or tenant if there is no agent) must deduct the landlord's tax from the rent at the basic-rate and make payment on his behalf.

Notice. A formal process telling the tenant that their tenancy will end on a predetermined date, which may include details about the landlord's intention to seek possession through the court if the tenant fails to vacate.

Permanent label. All new furniture (except those mentioned under **display label** above) must have a permanent label fixed to it, describing the product's compliance with the 1988 Regulations and information about the foam content.

Prescribed form. A term given that demands some forms and/or notices must have a layout and/or wording that conforms with the legislation describing it. For example, a landlord's **Notice to Quit** has to contain certain information, without which it may be considered invalid by the court.

Pre-tenancy determination. Those who qualify for housing benefit can request a pre-tenancy determination (PTD) when considering a tenancy from a private landlord. A PTD is arranged by the local authority via the rent officer service and provides an indication of the maximum benefit that will be paid for the property. A recipient is then aware of whether the entire rent or only a portion of it will be covered. PTDs are applied to the property, not the H/b claimant, and are valid for 12 months.

Quiet enjoyment. The tenant's statutory right to occupy and use the property within the terms agreed and without interference or disturbance.

Reinstatement. Restoring something to its former state. With regard to property letting, this usually means repairing to make-good or replacing or renewing to a level of quality commensurate with when it was first supplied, i.e. at the start of tenancy.

Rent Officer. The Rent Officer Service is an Executive Agency of the Department of the Environment, Transport and the Regions, and operates through local authorities. The Rent Officer's main functions are to undertake Fair Rent evaluations for regulated and secure tenancies, to make pre-tenancy determinations for housing benefit, and advise local authorities about the effects on rent of Housing Renovation Grant applications.

Rent. Rent is normally a sum of money paid under contract, by a tenant, in return for possession of a property for a period of time. However, rent *can* mean something other than legal tender, for example, it may be agreed that a service is provided instead.

Resident. A resident landlord is one who lives in the same building as their tenant. An exception exists where the landlord lives in a purpose-built block of flats and lets one of the other flats in the same block.

Roll-over relief. The term refers to delaying the payment of Capital Gains Tax by reinvesting the profit made from the sale of one business into another.

Security of tenure. The right of the tenant to **quiet enjoyment** of the property for a determined or indefinite period of time.

Service charge. A mandatory charge made by a landlord or headlessor to the tenant or leaseholder.

Set-off. Tenants have a right, under certain conditions, to withhold rent for repairs that have been requested but not conducted. They can set off the appropriate sum to finance the repairs they have had to arrange themselves as a result.

Severally liable. Joint tenants are usually described as being severally liable. This means each tenant is equally responsible and accountable for the other tenants' actions. For example, if one tenant fails to pay rent, it is the same as if all tenants had failed to make the payment.

Short assured tenancy. A tenancy in Scotland under the Housing (Scotland) Act 1988 and similar to (but not the same as) the assured shorthold tenancy in England and Wales.

Sitting tenant. Someone whose occupation of a property is protected by law, even if the property is sold to another person.

Stamp duty. A government tax associated with property documents.

Statutory periodic tenancy. A statutory periodic tenancy (SPT) is created automatically at the end of an assured shorthold tenancy (AST) if either the landlord or tenant do nothing to prevent it. An SPT has the same terms as the prior AST but runs according to the periodic nature of rent payments, for example, month to month.

Statutory protection. The rights and security afforded to both landlord and tenant by primary legislation under Acts of

Law (as distinct from contrary terms that may be written into a tenancy agreement).

Sub-let. The term given to a tenant who lets the property (or part of it) to another tenant.

Succession. The right of a spouse or a family member who satisfies the criteria to continue enjoying occupation of a property, after the tenant has died. Family members *can* include unmarried partners, regardless of gender, if a court interprets the relationship accordingly.

Surrender. A tenant who voluntarily relinquishes their tenancy in agreement with the landlord.

Survey. The examination of a building and the identification of faults and/or an appraisal of current market value.

Template. A stencil or pattern used as a guide to create a similar product or consummate document.

Tenancy agreement. A contractually binding agreement between landlord and tenant, detailing the terms under which a property is provided. Verbal agreements should be avoided as they give rise to doubt and the terms will be difficult to prove in court.

Tenancy. The exclusive possession of property usually granted for a period of time and in return for rent.

Tenant. Someone with a legal right to occupy and/or use a property according to certain terms and conditions.

Unfurnished. There is no legal definition of what constitutes an unfurnished property. Generally it means the dwelling is supplied without furnishings, fittings, appliances and equipment, but may include fixtures.

Vacant possession. The property is handed over at completion with no one occupying it and no one having any legal right to occupy it.

Vendor. The person selling the property.

Void period. The period between tenancies when the property is empty and there is therefore no rental income.

White goods. A term that refers to kitchen appliances such as an automatic washing-machine, fridge-freezer, dish-washer and cooker.

Yield. The annual rate of return on investment expressed as a percentage.

Useful Information

USEFUL CONTACT INFORMATION

ARLA (Association of Residential Letting Agents), Maple House, 53–55 Woodside Road, Amersham, Bucks HP6 6AA. Tel: 0845 345 5752. Website: www.arla.co.uk

British Insurance Brokers Association, 14 Bevis Marks, London EC3A 7NT. Tel: (020) 7623 9043.

Website: www.biba.org.uk

British Standards Institute, 389 Chiswick High Road, London. W4 4AL. Tel: (020) 8996 9000.

Website: bsi-global.com

British Urban Regeneration Association, Room 10, 4th Floor, Glen House, Stag Place, London SW1E 5AG. Tel: 0800 0181 260. Website: www.bura.org.uk

CORGI (Council of Registered Gas Installers), 1 Elmwood, Chineham Business Park, Crockford Lane, Basingstoke, Hants RG24 8WG. Tel: (01256) 372200.

Website: www.corgi-gas.com

Court Service (Information and Advice), Southside, 105 Victoria Street, London SW1E 6QT. Tel: (020) 7210 2266.

Website: www.courtservice.gov.uk

DWP (Department for Work and Pensions) formally the DSS, Correspondence Unit, Room 540, The Adelphi, 1–11 John Adam Street, London WC2N 6HT. Tel: (020) 7712 2171. Website: www.dwp.gov.uk

DTI (Department of Trade and Industry) Publications Unit, DTI Publications Orderline. ADMAIL 528, London

SW1W 8YT. Tel: (020) 7215 6024.

Website: www.dti.gov.uk

DTLR (Department for Transport, Local Government and the Regions) Free Literature, P O Box 236, Wetherby LS23 7NB. Tel: 0870 1226 236.

Website: www.housing.odpm.gov.uk/order/index.htm

Federation of Small Businesses, Sir Frank Whittle Way, Blackpool Business Park, Blackpool, Lancashire FY4 2FE. Tel: (01253) 336000. Website: www.fsb.org.uk

FSO (The Financial Services Authority), 25 The North Colonnade, Canary Wharf, London E14 5HS. Tel: 0845 606 1234. Website: www.fsa.gov.uk/consumer

Health and Safety Executive, Rose Court, 2 Southwark Bridge, London SE1 9HS. Tel: 08701 545500.

Website: www.hse.gov.uk

HMSO (Her Majesty's Stationery Office), St Clements House, 2–16 Colegate, Norwich NR3 1BQ. Tel: 0870 600 5522. Website: www.hmso.gov.uk

Information Commissioner (Data Protection), Wycliffe House, Water Lane, Wilmslow, Cheshire SK9 5AF. Tel: (01625) 545 745. Website: www.dataprotection.gov.uk

Inland Revenue, St Mungo's Road, Town Centre, Cumbernauld, Glasgow G70 5TR. Tel: (01236) 736121.

Website: www.inlandrevenue.gov.uk

Leasehold Advisory Service, 70–74 City Road, London EC1Y 2BJ. Tel: 0845 345 1993.

Website: www.lease-advice.org.uk

Mediation UK, Alexander House, Telephone Avenue, Bristol BS1 4BS. Tel: (0117) 904 6661.

Website: www.mediationuk.org.uk

National Association of Citizens Advice Bureaux, Myddelton House, 115–123 Pentonville Road, London N1 9LZ. Tel:

(020) 7833 2181. Website: www.nacab.org.uk

Office of Fair Trading, Fleetbank House, 2–6 Salisbury Square, London EC4Y 8JX. Tel: 08457 224499. Website: www.oft.gov.uk

OFWAT (Office of Water Services – Regulator of the Water Industry), Centre City Tower, 7 Hill Street, Birmingham B5 4UA. Tel: (0121) 625 1300. Website: www.ofwat.gov.uk

Rent Service, The, 1st Floor, Clifton House, 87–113 Euston Road, London NW1 2RA. Tel: (020) 7388 4838. Website: www.therentservice.gov.uk

Royal Institute of Chartered Surveyors (RICS), Contact Centre, Surveyor Court, Westwood Way, Coventry CV4 8JE. Tel: 0870 333 1600. Website: www.rics.org

Scottish Executive Development Department (Free Leaflets), Victoria Quay, Edinburgh EH6 6QQ. Tel: 08457 741 741. Website: www.scotland.gov.uk/housing/leaflets

Trading Standards, 4–5 Hadleigh Business Centre, 351 London Road, Hadleigh, Essex SS17 2BT. Tel: 0870 872 9000. Website: www.trading standards.gov.uk

TRANSCO (Gas Emergency Service), 31 Homer Road, Solihull, West Midlands B91 3LT. Tel: (0121) 626 4431 (emergency 0800 111999). Website: www.transco.uk.com

TSO (The Stationery Office), 51 Nine Elms Lane, London SW8 5DR. Tel: (020) 7873 8787. Website: www.tso.co.uk

Valuation Office (Council Tax), Chief Executives Office, New Court, 48 Carey Street, London. WC2A 2JE. Tel: (020) 7506 1700. Website: www.voa.gov.uk

LANDLORDS' ASSOCIATIONS

Eastern Landlords' Association, 44–48 Sackville Place, Magdalen Street, Norwich, Norfolk. Tel: (01603) 767101. Website: www.easternlandlords.org.uk

Fife Landlords' Association, 16 Coldstream Crescent, Leven, Fife KY8 5TD. Tel: (01333) 302356.

Website: www.fife-landlords-association.co.uk

Gateshead Private Landlords' Association, Commercial & Consumer Services, Regent Street, Gateshead, Tyne & Wear NE8 1HH. Tel: (0191) 4333967.

Website: www.gpla.co.uk

Incorporated Association of Landlords, Suite 12, Kilmun Court, Kilmun PA23 8SF. Tel: 0870 745 3077.

Website: www.ial.org.uk

Merseyside & Wirral Landlords' Association, Freepost NWW131A, PO Box 80, Crosby, Liverpool L23 6YJ. Tel: (0151) 286 2146.

Website: www.merseyworld.com/mwla

National Federation of Residential Landlords, Executive Office, PO Box 4840, Poole BH15 3WD. Tel: 0845 456 0357. Website: www.nfrl.org.uk

National Landlords' Association, 78 Tachbrook Street, London SW1V 2NA. Tel: 0870 241 0471.

Website: www.landlords.org.uk

North East Lincolnshire Landlords' Association, PO Box 347, Cleethorpes, NE Lincolnshire DN35 0XS. Tel: (01472) 354801. Website: www.beehive.thisisgrimsby.co.uk/default.asp?WCI = SiteHome&ID = 1710

North Wales Private Landlords' Association, NWPLA, PO Box 36, Rhyl LL18 1ZD. Tel: (01745) 330792.

North West Landlords' Association Limited, 108 Market Street, Westhoughton, Bolton, Lancashire BL5 3AZ.

Residential Landlords' Association, 1 Roebuck Lane, Sale, Manchester M33 7SY. Tel: (0161) 962 0010.

Website: www.rla.org.uk

Scottish Association of Landlords, Gladstone House, 6a Mill Lane, Edinburgh EH6 6TJ. Tel: (0131) 555 5911. **Website: www.scottishlandlords.com**

Southern Private Landlords' Association, PO Box 2883, Brighton BN1 1PB. Tel: (01273) 600847. **Website: www.spla.co.uk**

South of Scotland Private Landlords' Association, 23a Galloway Street, Dumfries DG2 7TL. Tel: (01387) 253661. **Website: www.swslandlords.co.uk**

South Yorkshire Landlords' Association, The Moorings, 8 Dunniwood Reach, Bessacarr, Doncaster DN4 7AS. Tel: (01302) 533131. **Website: www.rkharris.co.uk/syorkshirelandlords**

Yorkshire Coast Residential Landlords' Association, PO Box 227, Scarborough YO11 1YW. Tel: 0845 330 4582. **Website: www.ycrla.com**

ADDITIONAL WEBSITES

Of the thousands of sites available online, these are some of the most useful for landlords:

www.landlord-law.co.uk Superb legal information resource for landlords with access to tenancy documents.

www.landlordzone.co.uk My personal favourite – contains a wealth of information and helpful resources.

www.letlink.co.uk The Letting Centre site has a vast amount of valuable information and advice.

www.lettingnetwork.com Links to other sites of interest to landlords.

www.lettingzone.com Contact details for landlord associations throughout the UK.

www.scottishlaw.org.uk/lawscotland/landlord.html View the laws and regulations affecting landlords in Scotland.

www.scottish-letting-agency.com Lots of useful information for Scottish landlords.

www.themoneycentre.co.uk Advice and analysis of the best buy-to-let mortgages available.

www.themovechannel.com Guidance for novice landlords and resources for anyone moving home.

Index